TIME-BARRED ACTIONS

TIME-BARRED ACTIONS

SECOND EDITION

Edited by

FRANCESCO BERLINGIERI O.B.E
Former Professor of Maritime Law at the University of Genoa
Honorary President, Comité Maritime International
Advocate, Senior Partner, Studio Legale Berlingieri

FOREWORD BY ALLAN PHILIP, PRESIDENT OF THE COMITÉ MARITIME INTERNATIONAL

PUBLISHED UNDER THE AUSPICES OF THE COMITÉ MARITIME INTERNATIONAL

COMITE MARITIME INTERNATIONAL
CMI

LLP

LONDON NEW YORK HAMBURG HONG KONG
LLOYD'S OF LONDON PRESS LTD.
1993

Lloyd's of London Press Ltd.
Legal Publishing Division
27 Swinton Street, London WC1X 9NW

USA AND CANADA
Lloyd's of London Press Inc.
Suite 308, 611 Broadway
New York, NY 10012 USA

GERMANY
Lloyd's of London Press GmbH
59 Ehrenbergstrasse
2000 Hamburg 50, Germany

SOUTH EAST ASIA
Lloyd's of London Press (Far East) Ltd.
Room 1101, Hollywood Centre
233 Hollywood Road
Hong Kong

First published in Great Britain in 1984
Second edition 1993

British Library Cataloguing in Publication Data
A catalogue record for this book
is available from the British Library

ISBN 1-85044-525-7

Promenade Graphics, Gloucester
Printed in Great Britain by
WBC Ltd., Bridgend,
Mid Glamorgan

FOREWORD

In 1984 the late Kaj Pineus compiled the first edition of this book for the Comité Maritime International. The book is a very useful tool for maritime lawyers and it was, therefore, the wish of the Comité Maritime International that a revised edition should be put at the disposal of the legal maritime community. I was, therefore, very pleased when Professor Francesco Berlingieri accepted to undertake the revision. The result is a very extensive treatment of the subject on a comparative basis. It is based upon co-operation between Francesco Berlingieri and representatives of the National Associations of the Comité Maritime International. Without Francesco Berlingieri's energy in holding his collaborators to their task and his ability to get things done this new edition would never have come about.

July 1993 ALLAN PHILIP

QUESTIONNAIRE FOR THE SECOND EDITION OF THE BOOK "TIME-BARRED ACTIONS"

I. LEGAL NATURE OF THE TIME BAR PERIOD

State whether the lapse of the period affects the substantive right or the action. In the latter case, state whether or not the right can be enforced thereafter and how. In view of the fact that time-bar is an expression which seems to refer to the barring of the right of action, I have deemed it convenient to refer throughout the questionnaire to "time-bar/extinction", where by "extinction" I intend to refer to the extinction of the right.

II. TIME-BAR/EXTINCTION PERIODS IN RESPECT OF VARIOUS TYPES OF MARITIME CLAIMS

Please indicate the length of the period and also indicate when the period commences to run.

A. Tort Claims

1. Collision.
2. Pollution.
3. Other damage to the environment.
4. Damage to third parties at sea (e.g. to a swimmer) or ashore (e.g. damage to a port installation, or to persons).
5. Damage to the salved ship during salvage operations (this may also give rise to a contract claim).

B. Contract Claims

1. Shipbuilding and ship repairs.
2. Supplies to ship.
3. Agency agreements.
4. Terminal operations (loading, stowage, unstowage, unloading, storage, etc).

5. Contract of affreightment except loss of or damage to cargo (*Note: all types of breach of contract of affreightment (demise charters, time charters, voyage charters, tonnage agreements, carriage of cargo in a general ship must be considered, such as: failure to make the ship available, delays in the time of delivery, unjustified withdrawal, unseaworthiness, payment of freight, damage to the ship, demurrage and dispatch, etc*).

6. Loss of or damage to cargo under charterparties and bills of lading.

7. Contracts of carriage of passengers (except death or personal injury and loss of or damage to baggage): e.g. payment of fare, non-performance of the voyage, delays, etc.

8. Death of or personal injury to passengers and loss of or damage to baggage under a contract of carriage of passengers by sea.

9. Insurance: all claims under a contract of insurance including claims for payment of premiums and insurance indemnities, abandonment (if a special time limit is prescribed).

10. Reinsurance.

11. General average.

12. Salvage.

III. TIME-BAR/EXTINCTION PERIODS FOR SECURITIES

Note: The time-bar/extinction period that must be considered is that relating to the security itself, and not to the credit or claim secured thereby.

1. Mortgages and hypothèques.
2. Maritime liens.
3. Possessory and other liens.
4. Other charges.

IV. SUSPENSION OR INTERRUPTION OF THE TIME-BAR AND EXTINCTION PERIODS

The period of time after the lapse of which the action is barred or the right is extinguished may be suspended or interrupted. The difference between suspension or interruption consists of that in case of suspension the original time limit continues to run after the period of suspension, whilst in case of interruption a new period commences to run anew from the date of the interruption. It is requested that you state what your national law is on the following matters.

1. Whether there are any statutory provisions in respect of the suspension of time-bar or extinction periods.

2. Whether the parties may agree on the suspension of the time-bar period and, if so, how.

3. Whether the time bar may be extended by court.

4. What are the statutory rules on the interruption of the time-bar or extinction periods. State how the running of the time may be interrupted, viz:

(i) by commencement of a judicial proceeding and when the proceeding is deemed to be commenced;
(ii) by other types of action, such as application for a summary judgment or of an injunction, by the arrest or attachment of a property of the debtor, etc;
(iii) by a notice of default or formal request of payment;
(iv) in any other manner.

5. If the dispute must be submitted to arbitration, when the running of the time is interrupted, viz: at the time of notice of appointment of the first arbitrator, at the time the arbitral tribunal accepts the appointment, etc.

6. Whether the commencement of an action before a court that does not have jurisdiction to decide the dispute has the effect of interrupting the running of the time or not.

7. Whether in case a proceeding is abandoned or discontinued, the time commences to run again and, if so, from when.

CONTENTS

INTRODUCTION*

An attorney will not always win his case. How could he? He is not expected to. It will not be held against him unless it happens because he had missed a time bar. To avoid that calamity in international maritime affairs, the Comité Maritime International (CMI) thought it wise to endeavour to show what the respective time-bar rules are in various countries and how they work.

Following a request by Lloyd's of London Press, the CMI agreed to assist in the preparation of a second edition of *Time-Barred Actions* by the late Kaj Pineus. I was asked by the President of the CMI, Professor Allan Philip, to take care of the editing of the new edition and deemed it convenient to draw up and circulate a new questionnaire, partly based on that originally prepared by Kaj Pineus and partly dealing with additional problems relating to time bars.

RATIONALE OF TIME BARS

The fundamental reason why a claim will lapse with time, a principle accepted everywhere, is the wish to finalise matters once and for all. Claims must not be allowed to grow too old; evidence is then likely to have disappeared. A party should feel safe that no valid claims will have to be entertained after a certain date. A claimant should not be allowed to come forward with his claim too late when evidence to rebut it is no longer available to the would-be debtor.

PRACTICAL IMPACT

The practical impact of time-bar rules will be different depending on their length. If the general time-bar period in respect to claims is long, say 30 years as in the Netherlands or 10 years as in Finland and Sweden, the practical effect will be manifestly less than if the two-year period allotted

* Much of this introduction is based on the introduction to the first edition for which acknowledgement must be given to the late Kaj Pineus.

to claimants under the Collision Convention of 1910 applies. Thus, in maritime affairs where the time bars are comparatively short, their effects will be marked. You might easily miss the boat!

CONVENTIONS AND NATIONAL LAW

Where Conventions govern the rules regarding time bars in certain circumstances or for particular claims the provisions of the Convention are laid out at the beginning of the relevant section (e.g. the Salvage Convention 1989 is highlighted under section C-12 on salvage).

WHETHER EXTENSIONS OF A TIME BAR ARE PERMISSIBLE

Can the parties agree to extend a time bar? In some jurisdictions they can, provided such agreement is reached after the claim arose and not before. Is court action, in one form or another, necessary to stop the time bar from running out? In some jurisdictions it is. Is a simple reminder to the debtor enough? This is accepted in some jurisdictions but not in respect of most of the claims dealt with in this survey. Can a court of law extend the relevant time-bar period? Under the doctrine of laches in the USA this is possible under certain circumstances. Thus, there is no uniform answer to the important question of how to stop the time-bar period from running out.

INTERRUPTION AND SUSPENSION OF THE TIME BAR

Different rules exist in the various systems of law as regards the possible suspension and interruption of the time bar and as regards the effects of any such suspension or interruption.

The fundamental difference between suspension and interruption seems to be that whilst suspension causes the clock to stop for a certain period of time and then the original time-bar period commences to run again, in case of interruption, from the date when the interruption takes place, a fresh time bar commences anew.

TERMINOLOGY

In the introduction to the first edition Kaj Pineus explained that although different terms are used to describe the situation where an action is lost by lapse of time, he deemed it convenient to use the neutral term *time bar* throughout the book. It has appeared from the replies to the new questionnaire, however, that not only does the legal nature of the "time bar" differ in a number of jurisdictions but in many jurisdictions, and more specifically in those governed by civil law, there are terms which have a different legal nature. For this reason it has been considered preferable to use, whenever possible, the terminology in force in the various jurisdictions, save that the term *prescription* in French, *prescripcion* in Spanish and *prescrizione* in Italian has been translated into English as *prescription* and that the verb "to prescribe" has also been used to describe the action of prescription. However, when the words used in the replies to the questionnaire were "time bars" such words have been left unaltered.

STRUCTURE OF THE NEW EDITION

In the first edition, the information received from the National Association was arranged in two ways. First, under each individual issue and, secondly, under each country. It has now been decided to adopt only the first format since reference to this book would be expected on encountering a particular situation or claim. It is hoped, in fact, that the reader will easily find all the information he may require in respect of any individual national legislation through the questionnaire, the table of contents and the index.

REPLIES AND ACKNOWLEDGEMENT

Replies to the questionnaire were received from the following Maritime Law Associations:

Argentina	Greece	Norway
Australia	Hong Kong	Poland
Canada	Ireland	Portugal
Chile	Israel	Spain
China	Italy	Sweden
Croatia	Japan	Switzerland
Denmark	Korea	Turkey
France	Malta	United Kingdom
Germany	Netherlands	United States

The various National Associations have given much attention and devoted much study to the many intricate problems raised in the questionnaire. This is, of course, in keeping with the traditions of the CMI. Still, it is felt proper to express my high appreciation of this work.

FRANCESCO BERLINGIERI

EDITOR'S NOTE

The reader's attention is drawn to the following list of countries from which replies to the questionnaire were not received.

Belgium
Brazil
Finland
India
Mexico
U.S.S.R
Venezuela

Consequently, the information included on these countries comprise their replies received on the original questionnaire in 1982. A word of caution is, therefore, necessary since the law in these countries may have changed in the meanwhile.

TABLE OF CASES

FRANCE

GREECE

ITALY

JAPAN

SPAIN

TABLE OF INTERNATIONAL CONVENTIONS

TABLE OF LEGISLATION

I

LEGAL NATURE OF THE TIME-BAR PERIOD

Argentina

The lapse of the period affects the action. The right that has not been exercised within the period fixed by the law cannot be enforced, but the obligation continues to exist as a "natural" obligation, and if the debtor pays the debt after the expiration of the period, he cannot claim reimbursement.

Australia

In New South Wales, the claimant's right of action for a debt or damages is extinguished on expiration of the limitation period (Limitation Act 1969 (NSW), s. 63(1)).

In Victoria, Queensland, Tasmania and the Northern Territory, if the owner of personal property (that is, goods or a ship) has been wrongfully dispossessed of the property, or if the property has been wrongfully detained by another, the owner's right to the property is extinguished on expiration of the limitation period.[1]

A cause of action for loss of or damage to goods carried under bills of lading, to which the Hague or Hague-Visby Rules apply, is extinguished on expiration of the limitation period. However, where an order is made by a court to extend the time within which arbitration proceedings may be commenced, a cause of action barred by the Hague or Hague-Visby Rules is thereby revived.

In the other Australian jurisdictions, and for all other kinds of action in the jurisdictions mentioned above, lapse of the limitation period bars the claimant's right to bring an action, but does not extinguish the right itself. The claimant may enforce the right by any other avenues that may be available, for example, by exercising a possessory lien.

1. Limitation of Actions Act 1958 (Vic), s. 6(2); Limitation of Actions Act 1974 (Qld), s. 12(2); Limitation Act 1974 (Tas), s. 6(2); Limitation Act 1981 (NT), s. 19(2).

Canada

Unless specifically provided, lapse of the period affects the action and not the substantive right. The right can be enforced thereafter only by renunciation by the defendant of either the elapsed time or of the defence of the time bar itself.

Chile

Under Chilean law, prescription is a mode of extinction of actions and rights resulting from the failure to exercise such actions and rights during a certain period of time when the other requisites (inertia or renunciation by the titular) are present. The extinction operates both in respect of the substantive right and of the action.

Croatia

By the expiration of the time-bar period the obligation is not extinguished. The creditor can claim performance of such an obligation by commencing the action, but the debtor can take exception on the ground that the action is time-barred. The court may not treat an action as time-barred on its own initiative (Article 360, paragraph 3 of the Law of Obligations 1978). The debtor cannot waive the time-bar before the time-bar period expires (Article 365 of the Law of Obligations 1978).

France

The legal nature of the prescription is still debated by legal writers. The prevailing opinion, however, is that the prescription extinguishes the action, not the right.

Germany

In German law there is a clear distinction between *Verjährungsfrist* (prescription period) and *Ausschlussfrist* (extinction period). *Verjährungsfrist* constitutes an *Einrede* (defence)—that is a right to refuse performance without affecting the substantive right. The substantive right remains as *causa* for any later performance of the debtor irrespective of *Verjährung* so that the creditor would not obtain an unjust enrichment. *Ausschlussfrist* constitutes an *Einwendung* (objection)—that is the right to refuse performance for the reason that the substantive right is extinguished. If the debtor performs after the extinction of the right he performs without causa and becomes entitled to claim restitution. In court proceedings an *Einrede* is only to be considered if the debtor makes an explicit plea while an *Einwendung* is considered *ex officio*. Whether the time bar is a *Verjährungsfrist* or an *Ausschlussfrist* depends on the relevant statutory provision. In particular, in maritime cases the special rules of the relevant conventions are applicable.

Greece

The Greek Civil Code (Chapter X—Prescription and extinction periods) makes a distinction between prescription which extinguishes the action and extinction period which causes the extinction of the substantive right itself.

The above distinction is important in several respects:

(a) Only claims may be prescribed, whereas rights may be extinguished.

(b) Prescription is set only by law; by contrast, an extinction period may be set either by law or by contract.

(c) The right to invoke prescription can be waived, whereas a waiver of an extinction period is not possible. As a result, a prescribed claim may be enforced either when the right to invoke the prescription has been waived or when it is not invoked in the court by the party entitled thereto or, in theory, when it is wrongly invoked. In addition, when the debtor has performed the obligations which arise from a prescribed claim, he is not entitled to invoke the invalidity of the above performance since the prescription of the right of action does not affect the substantive right itself.

Ireland

The lapse of the period only takes away the remedy by action. It leaves the substantive right unaffected. For instance, a security may be enforced even though given in respect of a barred debt. However, where a charterparty incorporates the provisions of the Hague Rules that any suit for loss or damage should be brought within one year, the claim is entirely extinguished after the year if no proceedings have been brought.

An inextinguishable right can be enforced after the lapse of time, in the case of disability, where there has been an acknowledgement or part payment or in cases of fraud or mistake.

Israel

Under the Limitation Act 1958, limitation does not affect the substantive right, but only the remedy of action in court. The right can still be asserted as set-off or counterclaim in an action brought for a claim which has not become time-barred (or against which the time bar is not pleaded), provided that both claims arise out of the same set of circumstances. Limitation does not prevent the creditor from pursuing the remedy of execution of mortgages, pawns or liens securing the right.

Italy

Whilst the Italian Civil Code of 1865 did not make clear whether the lapse of time caused the extinction of the substantive right or merely of the action, the Civil Code of 1942 makes the position clear. Article 2934, under the rubric "Extinction of rights", so provides in its first paragraph:

> Any right is extinguished by prescription when the holder thereof does not exercise it for the time determined by the law.

Therefore the lapse of the period takes away the right itself.

Japan

The time, the lapse of which affects the right or the action, is under classified Japanese law as follows:

(a) Prescription (*Jiko*), and
(b) Period of exclusion (*Joseki Kikan*).

For both, the lapse of the time causes the extinction of the substantive right. However, whilst the prescription must be invoked by the debtor and cannot be considered by the court on its own initiative, the lapse of the period of exclusion must be established by the court, whether or not the exception is taken by the debtor.

A further difference between prescription and exclusion periods relates to the possibility of interrupting the running of the former, but not of the latter (see pages 177–178 below).

Korea

A clear distinction between prescription period (*Verjährungsfrist*) and extinction period (*Ausschlussfrist*) exists in the law of the Republic of Korea. The lapse of the prescription period or extinction period extinguishes the substantive right itself; however, they differ in the following respects:

(a) In court proceedings, the lapse of the prescription period must be raised as a defence by the defendant pursuant to Article 188 of the Code of Civil Procedure (*Verhandlungsmaxime*), while the extinction period is considered by the court *ex officio*.
(b) The prescription period has retroactive effect from the date on which it began to run, while the extinction period does not have retroactive effect.

(c) Generally, it is set out in the relevant statutory provisions whether the time-bar period is a prescription period or an extinction period.
(d) There are statutory provisions for suspension or interruption of the prescription period, but the extinction period runs without suspension or interruption (see pages 169–170 and 184–185 below).

If a debtor performs his obligation after the lapse of the prescription period, he is not entitled to claim reimbursement of the money paid, while in case of the extinction period, he is entitled to claim reimbursement.

Malta

Section 2107(2) of the Civil Code defines extinctive prescription as "a mode of releasing oneself from an action, when the creditor has failed to exercise his right for a time specified by law". Extinctive prescription is thus a plea in bar of the action, but not of the right.

The ordinary extinctive prescription according to Maltese law is that of 30 years and of 40 years in respect of Church property (Civil Code, s. 2143). There are then shorter prescriptions for specified actions. In commercial matters, the general rule is that the period specified by law for acquiring a prescription is shorter than that specified with respect to civil matters. Section 2156(f) of the Civil Code provides that actions for the payment of any debt arising from commercial transactions, unless such debt is, under the civil or any other law, barred by the lapse of a shorter period or unless it results from a public deed, are barred by the lapse of five years.

Netherlands

The law of carriage, regulated in Book 8 of the Civil Code, in principle only recognizes time-bar (prescription) periods, i.e. the lapse of the period affects the right of action. The law contains extinction periods, i.e. the lapse of the period affects the substantive right, only where treaties or the required harmony with such treaties necessitate such.

After the expiration of the time-bar period, a "natural obligation" remains, i.e. an obligation which cannot be enforced at law. A time-barred claim can however still be enforced in the following cases:

—performance of an obligation can be suspended until the time-barred claim against the other party is paid;
—the right of retention of and the right of pledge on a moveable thing or on a promissory note payable to bearer or order may still be exercised;
—the right of set-off continues to exist.

Norway

The lapse of the period affects the substantive right of the claim. However, it is, of course, fully permissible for the debtor to pay a claim even if it has become time-barred. In other words, it will not be considered as a gift from the debtor if he pays a time-barred claim. The importance of this appears in relation to for instance his other creditors and heirs, etc.

To a certain extent, a time-barred claim may also be set-off against a non-time-barred claim provided that the right to set-off is expressly agreed, or the claim and the counter-claim are originating from the same agreement, and also provided that the counter-claim has arisen before the claim became time-barred. The following example illustrates the point. A seller's claim for the purchase price is time-barred. The purchaser is claiming compensation for defects in the goods. Provided that the purchaser's claim for compensation has arisen before the claim for the purchase price became time-barred, the seller is entitled to set-off his claim against the purchaser's claim for the purchase price, even if the latter is time-barred.

Poland

The Polish Maritime Code of 1961 does not contain any general rules governing prescription periods. This Code regulates prescription periods in respect of specific types of maritime claims only. Generally it governs legal relations incident to maritime shipping. In the absence of provisions of the Maritime Code, the provisions of the Civil Code of 1964 are applicable to the civil law relations incident to maritime shipping. So prescription periods in respect of maritime claims are governed by the general provisions of the Civil Code unless there exist specific provisions in the Maritime Code governing a given type of maritime claim.

According to Article 118 of the Civil Code, the prescription period is 10 years, but for claims concerning periodical performance, the period is three years unless a specific provision prescribes a shorter term.

Portugal

Portuguese law knows two different types of time bar: "*prescriçao*" (prescription) and "*caducidade*" (déchéance). Conceptually, *caducidade* refers to the exercise of a right in due time, *viz.* the commencement of an action which is a right different from that, which by means of such action, it is intended to enforce.

The main difference between *caducidade* and prescription lies in the difference between the notions of exercise of the right and the right itself. That is, *caducidade*, as mentioned, causes the extinction of the right; prescription causes the extinction of the action, but not of the right.

Since the conceptual distinction between the two legal terms is sometimes not easy, the Civil Code, Art. 298, no. 2 sets out the rule according to which, when by law or by will of the parties, a right must be exercised within a certain time limit, the rules on *caducidade* are applicable, unless the law expressly refers to prescription for that particular case.

Spain

Extinctive prescription is regulated in Spanish law by the Civil Code (Articles 1930–1939 and 1961–1975). These rules have a general and supplementary value and are, therefore, applicable to all kinds of rights and actions whenever there is no special rule in other bodies of law.

The Commercial Code (Codigo de Comercio) contains a small group of special rules applicable to actions arising out of "commercial contracts", although it also includes the action for collision (see Articles 942–954 of the Commercial Code). Since most maritime contracts are considered commercial contracts, the rules of the Commercial Code are frequently the ones to apply in this field of law. However, the Civil Code rules on prescription always have a supplementary value (see Articles 943 and 2 of the Commercial Code).

Prescription rules of the Commercial Code refer only to "actions". The same occurs in Articles 1961–1975 of the Civil Code. However, Article 1930 of the Civil Code makes clear that extinction affects both, the right and the action. Therefore it may be said that the lapse of the period takes away the right itself. And this conclusion is also valid as regards special rules for commercial contracts. However, once the right is extinguished because of prescription, an action can still be brought. This is so because prescription is a benefit which has to be specifically pleaded by the defendant. The judge will not apply prescription on his own initiative.

Sweden

The position according to general Swedish law on time limits is that it is only the right of action that becomes affected by the time bar. The substantive right, in effect the claim itself, therefore, continues to exist as before.

After such time when the right to take action has become time-barred, the substantive right can still be invoked in the following cases:

(a) *Set-offs*: A claim which is time-barred can still be used for the purpose of a set-off. No regard will in such a situation be taken to the fact that all legal actions, previously available to enforce the claim, have become time-barred. However, it is disputed if a claim subject to a short time bar (one or two years) when time-barred may be used for set-off against a claim subject to a longer time bar (e.g. 10 years, according to the general rule of the Swedish Statute 1981 on time bars).

(b) *Right of pledge/right of lien*: These rights are unaffected by the fact that the claim, which in the first instance gave rise to them, has become time-barred.

(c) *Condictio indebiti*: If a debtor pays a debt which has become time-barred, he will not be able to recover what he has paid.

Maritime law

Section 347 of the Swedish Maritime Code, which contains rules for the determination of the length of the various time-bar periods, states that a maritime claim *ceases to exist* after the expiration of the time limit set out therein. According to legal writers this provision should be understood to mean that the substantive right is extinguished. The remedy of set-off etc. would therefore not be available.

Switzerland

Swiss law knows a distinction between the "*Verjährungsfrist*" (prescription period) and the "*Verwirkungsfrist*" (extinction period).

While the institute of the prescription merely affects the right of action, the lapse of an extinction period affects the substantive right. Thus, where the extinction applies the claimant will have no rights after the time has lapsed and the judge will recognize that fact *ex officio*, i.e. without an objection from the defendant to that effect.

This situation is different where the prescription period applies, in this case it is left to the defendant to invoke and plead the objection of the time bar. After the lapse of time the claimant has lost the possibility of enforcing the claim against the intent of the defendant, but he has not lost the claim itself. Thus, the creditor can, under certain circumstances, set-off a prescribed claim against claims of the debtor or otherwise invoke an objection of non-performance against the debtor claiming his part of the contractual rights.

Turkey

In Turkish law there are some important differences between prescription periods and extinction periods. Prescription periods provide a defence to the debtor. The debtor has the right to refuse performance without affecting the substantive right. The extinction periods on the contrary affect the right itself.

In court proceedings, a defence of prescription is not raised *ex officio*, but only if the debtor makes an explicit plea, whilst the lapse of an extinction period must be established *ex officio*. In contrast with the prescription period, the extinction period runs without suspension. It is interrupted only by instituting an action before a court or an arbitral tribunal.

United Kingdom

Under English law, the lapse of the limitation period only bars the remedy and does not extinguish the right itself.[2]

After the lapse of the limitation period prescribed by legislation, an action cannot be brought to enforce the right which has been infringed. However, time bar is a defence which must be specifically pleaded by the defendant (Rules of the Supreme Court, O. 18, R 8(1)). If a defendant omits through inadvertence to plead this defence, the court may still allow him to amend his pleadings to incorporate the defence if it considers that the plaintiff can be adequately compensated by an order for costs.[3]

Where the limitation period has lapsed, an action cannot be brought to enforce a debt. However the debt still remains due. If the creditor has a lien or charge for his debt, he can enforce the lien or charge even after the debt has become statute-barred.

United States

As a general rule, a statute of limitations is regarded as barring, or running against the remedy to which it applies and does not extinguish or impair the right, obligation, or cause of action. However, the barring of the remedy effectively bars the cause of action by making it inconsequential. This general rule is inapplicable where a statute gives a right of action, or creates a liability which did not exist at common law, and makes limitation of time an essential element in which case the running of the period bars the remedy and the right or cause of action conferred.[4]

Many maritime claims in the United States do not have specific statutory time bars. Instead, the equitable doctrine of laches is applied. Under laches, the court applies the time-bar period specified in the local state statute of limitations for the particular action or in an analogous federal statute, but the court is not bound to follow these applicable statutes of limitations. In deciding whether to time-bar an action under laches, the court also considers the cause of a plaintiff's delay in bringing suit, the amount of time that has passed, and any prejudice caused to the defendant by the delay. The court must then weigh all these factors and make an

2. The exceptions to this general rule are (a) in cases of successive conversions, Limitation Act 1980, s. 3(2); (b) in cases where the limitation period for the recovery of land has expired, Limitation Act 1980, s. 17; and (c) Consumer Protection Act 1987 cases, Limitation Act 1980, s. 11A(3).

3. *Harnett* v. *Fisher* [1927] A.C. 573.

4. 54 Corpus Juris Secundum, para. 11.

equitable decision. However, in practice, the court usually just applies the state statute of limitations or the analogous federal statute of limitations. Laches is an affirmative defence under Rule 8(c) of the Federal Rules of Civil Procedure.[5]

Venezuela

In Venezuela, matters relating to extinctive prescription and extinction (*caducidade*) in maritime matters are fundamentally dealt with in the Commercial Code (Book Second, Title IX) which regulates all matters connected with maritime trade in general, and, supplemental thereto, in the Civil Code (Book Three, Title XXIV).

Even though the Commercial Code was amended in 1955, the part concerned with prescriptions and "*caducidade*" (and in fact, the whole of the part of the Code relating to maritime matters) dates back to the last century, and for such reason there are no express provisions in the national legislation in respect of recent matters.

The system of the Commercial Code in respect of prescription and "*caducidades*" may be outlined as follows:

(a) *Express prescriptions and "caducidades"*. These are laid down in various provisions in which the relevant time limits are determined for matters, which are expressly regulated.
(b) *Special prescription*. Article 893 contains a general norm whereby when no special time limit is established in respect of any given claim, the time limit of five years shall apply. Accordingly, in the absence of an express provision, in maritime matters the five-year prescription applies, but only in respect of claims arising out of matters regulated by the Second Book of the Commercial Code, which is the one devoted to Maritime Law.
(c) *Ordinary prescription*. The ordinary 10-year prescription applies in such cases as are not covered by the preceding paragraphs, *viz*. when an express statutory provision does not exist or when the special prescription of five years (Article 893) is not applicable. The prescription is contemplated in Article 132 of the Commercial Code, which is of a general character and is applicable to such cases as involve actions arising out of obligations of a mercantile nature and further in Article 1977 of the Civil Code, which applies in all other cases.

5. T. Schoenbaum, *Admiralty and Maritime Law* 156 (1987).

II

TIME-BAR PERIODS IN RESPECT OF VARIOUS TYPES OF MARITIME CLAIMS

A. INTRODUCTION—WHEN THE TIME-BAR PERIOD COMMENCES TO RUN

Finland

The general time limit provided for enforcing a claim or a debt is 10 years. This period of limitation applies whenever there is no special statute to bar the right of action earlier than after 10 years. The date from which time begins to run is normally the day on which a claim arises (e.g. damage occurs).

Maritime claims are subject to special time limits.

Germany

If there are no special rules, time-bar periods commence to run when the claim has arisen and has fallen due. In the case of contractual claims the period begins to run from the end of the year when the claim has arisen. For certain types of contract claims, special rules exist. In the case of damages the period of three years begins to run when the claim has arisen, i.e. when the damage occurs; in the case of tort claims the injured party's knowledge of the damage is an additional requirement.

India

As a general rule, time limits commence to run from the time when the cause of action arises.

Italy

Pursuant to Article 2935 of the Civil Code the prescription periods commence to run when the right may be enforced. This is a general rule applicable in all cases unless otherwise expressly stated.

Spain

While time-bar periods for maritime claims arising out of commercial contracts are mainly specified in the Commercial Code, collision is a special case which is also contained in the same Code. But the general rule for tort claims is contained in the Civil Code.

Further, the special rules contained in private maritime conventions which have been ratified by Spain also have to be taken into account and are part of the Spanish body of law.

Turkey

Generally prescription periods commence to run when the claim has fallen due. The extinction period applies only for cases of loss of or damage to, goods which are the subject of the contract of carriage by sea.

B. TORT CLAIMS

China

The general prescription period is two years. No prescription operates in respect of claims of the State for damage to, or loss of, its property caused through the operation or management by an unauthorized person (Article 170 of the Opinions of the People's Supreme Court).

India

The general time limit is three years.

Israel

Under the Limitation Act, 1958 the time bar for all the tort claims enumerated hereunder is seven years and the limitation period starts from the accrual of the cause of action.

Italy

The general rule, which is applicable unless otherwise expressly stated, is that tort claims are prescribed after five years from the date when the event has occurred (Article 2947 of the Civil Code). If, however, the occurrence is considered by the law as a crime and for such a crime a longer period is provided, the longer period also applies to the civil action.

Malta

The general rule is that actions for damages, which do not arise out of contractual obligations are barred after the lapse of two years (section 2153 of the Civil Code.) With regard to the prescription of civil actions for damages arising from criminal offences, the rules laid down in the Criminal Code relating to the prescription of criminal actions shall be observed. Nevertheless, any person who has stolen a thing, or who has become the possessor thereof by means of fraud, or who has received or bought such thing, knowing it to have been stolen or fraudulently acquired, cannot plead this defence, notwithstanding any lapse of time (section 2154 of the Civil Code).

Poland

According to Article 442, section 1 of the Civil Code, claims for repairs of damage caused by a tort are prescribed after a lapse of three years from the day on which a person who had suffered damage learned of it and of a person obliged to repair it.

In any event, however, a claim is prescribed after a lapse of 10 years from the day on which the event causing the damage occurred.

Under section 2 of Article 442, if damage results from a crime or offence, the claim for repair of damages is prescribed after a lapse of 10 years from the day when the crime was committed regardless of when the person who had suffered damage learned of it and of the person obliged to repair it.

Regarding tort claims the Maritime Code contains no specific provisions except for collision cases.

Spain

Unless otherwise provided for, the specific casualties contemplated below and actions for damages which do not arise out of contractual obligations (except Article 1902 and subsequent articles of the Civil Code) are barred after the lapse of one year. Time counts as of the day in which the tortious act or omission came to the knowledge of the person suffering damage (Article 1968.2 of the Civil Code). Once the liability has been established by a judgment, prescription for actions for execution starts as of the date of such judgment (Article 1971 of the Civil Code).

If, however, the occurrence amounts to a crime and the person suffering damage chooses not to claim damages in the criminal proceedings, the time begins to count only once such proceedings are terminated by judgment or by stay of proceedings (Articles 111 *et seq*. of the Ley de Enjuiciamiento Criminal).

Except as above, civil liability arising out of a criminal offence follows the general rules of extinctive prescription contained in the Civil Code (Article 117 of the Codigo Penal).

Turkey

The general prescription period is one year from the time when the person who sustains the damage becomes aware of the damage and of the person who caused it. The maximum period is 10 years from the day when the damage occurred (Article 60 of the Code of Obligations).

1. COLLISION

Uniform Rules

Article 7 of the 1910 Brussels Convention for the Unification of Certain Rules of Law with Respect to Collision between Vessels (1910 Collision Convention) provides that actions for recovery of damages are prescribed after two years from the date of the casualty. It also regulates the prescription period for action of recovery of the owner of one of the ships involved in the collision against the owner of the other ship, in case the former has paid in respect of claims for death and personal injuries a larger part than that which he ought to bear on the basis of the proportion of the fault of his ship. In such a case, the prescription period is one year from the date of payment.

In the unofficial English translation of the Convention, the words "se prescrivent" (are prescribed) have been translated by the words "are barred" and the word "prescriptions" (prescription periods) in the third paragraph have been translated by "periods of limitation".

The accuracy of this translation has been confirmed in more recent multilingual conventions such as the 1974 Athens Convention Relating to the Carriage of Passengers and their Luggage by Sea (1974 Athens Convention), article 16 and the United Nations Convention on the Carriage of Goods by Sea, 1978 (Hamburg Rules), article 20.

Article 7 then provides that the grounds upon which the periods of prescription are suspended or interrupted are determined by the law of the court where the case is tried. Although this general rule allows full freedom to Contracting States to legislate as regards suspension and interruption of prescription periods, the last paragraph of Article 7 allows Contracting States to provide in the national laws that the prescription periods are extended in cases where it has not been possible to arrest the defendant vessel in the territorial waters of the State in which the plaintiff has his domicile or his principal place of business. This is a specific case of suspension of the prescription period.

Argentina

The prescription period is two years from the date of the occurrence. The recourse action is prescribed after one year from the date of payment (Article 370 of the Ley de Navegacìon).

Australia

1. For ships on international and interstate voyages: the time bar period is two years (Navigation Act 1912 (Cth), s. 396(1)).

2. For ships on intrastate voyages the time bar periods are the following:

—New South Wales, Victoria, Tasmania and Northern Territory:
For *in personam* or *in rem* actions against the ship other than the one suffering the damage: two years.[1]
—Queensland and Western Australia:
For *in personam* actions, six years.[2]
For *in rem* actions, no limit.[3]
—South Australia:
Six years.[4]

(NB: In each jurisdiction, the period commences from the time when the damage was caused).

Belgium

1. Actions for the recovery of damages are barred after two years from the date of the casualty (Article 270 of the Commercial Code, Book II).

2. Actions for indemnity in respect of damages paid in relation to death or personal injuries are barred after one year from the date of payment (Article 270 of the Commercial Code, Book II).

Brazil

There is no special time limit in respect of claims for damages arising out of a collision and, therefore, the general twenty-year prescription period (Article 442 of the Commercial Code and Article 177 of the Civil Code) is applicable.

1. Limitation Act 1969 (NSW), s. 22(2); Limitation of Actions Act 1958 (Vic), s. 5(1)(a); Limitation Act 1974 (Tas), s. 8(2); Limitation Act 1981 (NT), s. 20(3).
2. Limitation of Actions Act 1974 (Qld), s. 10(1)(a); Limitation Act 1935 (WA) s. 38(1)(i)(vi).
3. Limitation of Actions Act 1974 (Qld) s. 10(6)(a).
4. Limitation of Actions Act 1936 (SA) s. 35(c).

Canada

Section 572(1) of the Canada Shipping Act 1936 provides a two-year prescription:

No action is maintainable to enforce any claim or lien against a vessel or its owners in respect of any damage or loss to another vessel, its cargo or freight, or any property on board the vessel, or for damages for loss of life or personal injuries suffered by any person on board that vessel, caused by the fault of the former vessel, whether that vessel is wholly or partly at fault, unless proceedings therein are commenced within two years from the date when the damage or loss or injury was caused.

Chile

The prescription period is two years starting from the date of the accident; or three years starting from the date of the accident, if the vessel liable could not be arrested or proceedings could not be commenced against her whilst she was within the waters subject to Chilean jurisdiction, on account of her having left such waters after the collision, without calling at any other Chilean port (Article 1249, No. 4 of the Commercial Code).

China

Claims regarding the right of recourse as provided for in Article 169, paragraph 3 of the Maritime Code, are time barred after one year from the date of payment.

Croatia

Claims for damage resulting from the collision are time barred after a period of two years from the date of the collision (Article 764, paragraph 1 of the Maritime Law). The right of recourse is time barred after one year (Article 764, paragraph 2 of the Maritime law) from the date:

(a) when the judgment determining the amount of joint and several liability becomes final;
(b) of payment, unless court proceedings have been instituted;
(c) the creditor learns of the insolvency of the debtor with the provision that the time-bar period may not be longer than two years from the date of payment or from the date the judgment becomes final—if request is made for the distribution of the assets of the insolvent debtor (Article 761, paragraph 2 of the Maritime Law). These periods can be extended after the claim has arisen by written agreement between the parties (Article 764, paragraph 3).

Denmark

The time-bar period is two years from the date when the damage was caused (section 291, subsection 1, rule 2 of the Danish Merchant Shipping Act).

Finland

The time-bar period is two years from the date when damage occurred. If anyone has paid in excess of his proportion of the damages for personal injury (joint debtors), he has the right to claim contribution, within one year from such payment.

France

The prescription period is two years from the collision (Law of 7 July 1967, Article 7). The time limit does not run if the ship liable cannot be arrested in French waters.

The recourse action by one of the ships, which has fully indemnified the victims, against the other ship, is prescribed one year after payment (Article 7, paragraph 2).

Germany

The time-bar period is two years as provided by the 1910 Collision Convention. Its legal nature is that of a *Verjährungsfrist*.[5]

Greece

Claims for damage caused to persons or property as a result of a collision between ships are prescribed after one year (Article 289, paragraph 6 of the Code of Private Maritime Law—Law 3816 of 1958) beginning (Article 291, paragraph 1 of the same Code) at the end of the year during which the prescription period commences to run.

The Aeropagus (the Supreme Court of Greece) by its judgment No. 8/1962 has decided that the above time limit applies to all claims whatsoever of any claimant against the shipowner or the operator in respect of loss of life or personal injury, total or partial loss of or damage to property, including the ship's total loss, as a result of a collision. However, claims against a person who is personally liable, because the damage is caused by his unlawful act, whether wilful or negligent, are prescribed after the lapse of five years from the time when the claimant knew of the damage and of the person liable to pay compensation (Article 937, section 1 of the Civil

5. See page 2.

Code). Furthermore, if the collision at the same time constitutes a punishable offence which according to criminal law is subject to a longer prescription, such a longer prescription applies instead of the five-year prescription period provided for in Article 937, section 1 of the Civil Code (Article 937, section 2 of the Civil Code).

In the event of collision between ships of different nationality belonging to States parties to the 1910 Collision Convention, ratified by Greece by virtue of law 3886/1911, claims arising therefrom are prescribed two years (Article 7 of the Covention) after the date of the collision.

Hong Kong

The time bar is two years from the date of the cause of action as under the 1910 Collision Convention.

India

The time limit is three years.

Ireland

The time-bar period is two years as provided by the 1910 Collision Convention.

Italy

The prescription period is two years as provided by the 1910 Collision Convention.

Japan

Although Japan ratified the 1910 Collision Convention the Japanese Commercial Code has not been amended in line with the Convention. Consequently:

(a) Claims arising out of collision between Japanese vessels are time-barred one year after the collision (Commercial Code, s. 798(1)). This period was qualified as prescription by the High Court of Cassation (*Daishinin*).[6]

(b) Claims arising out of collision between vessels belonging to contracting States are time-barred after two years from the date of the casualty (Articles 7 and 12 of the 1910 Collision Convention).

6. Judgment of 10 July 1922, Case No. (o) 698 of 1921.

Korea

The extinction period is two years, as provided by the 1910 Collision Convention that was adopted by the Commercial Code. The parties, however, may extend this period by agreement (Article 848 of the Commercial Code).

Malta

The time-bar period is two years from the date of the casualty as provided by the 1910 Collision Convention (Article 7). No action shall lie for damages occasioned by collision between vessels when the collision occurs in a place in which the master could institute proceedings, unless the master made his protest (section 545(c) of the Commercial Code).

Mexico

The prescription period is two years, as provided by the 1910 Collision Convention.

Netherlands

1. The time-bar period is two years as provided for by Article 7 of the Collision Convention (1910). For collisions not falling within the scope of the Convention, the time-bar period is also two years, commencing to run from the day following the day of the event, provided the action is not founded on a contract (Civil Code, Art. 8: 1790).

2. This period is extended when the vessel that is held liable cannot be attached within the state where the creditor resides or has its corporate domicile. The extension is restricted in two respects. The period never exceeds five years following the day of the collision. If it exceeds the aforesaid period of two years, it ends in any case three months following the day on which it became possible to arrest the vessel (Civil Code, Art. 8: 1792).

Norway

The time-bar period is two years from the day the damage was done.

Poland

Any claim in respect of compensation for damage caused by collision between vessels is prescribed at the expiration of two years from the day of the collision (Article 235 of the Maritime Code).

Portugal

Portugal ratified the 1910 Collision Convention. Therefore, in accordance with Article 7 of this Convention, the actions in respect of loss or damage caused by collision are prescribed if they are not commenced within two years from the date of the occurrence and the causes of interruption and suspension of the prescription are fixed by the law of the state in whose jurisdiction the action is brought.

When, according to Article 12, paragraph 2 of the Collision Convention this rule does not apply, the prescription period is three years from the date when the claimant becomes aware of his right (Article 498 no. 1 of the Civil Code).

Russia

Russia is a party to the 1910 Collision Convention and, therefore, the time limit for actions in respect of collision damages is two years and the time limit for action for indemnity is one year (Article 305 of the Merchant Shipping Code).

In cases not covered by the Collision Convention the general three-year time limit applies.

Spain

In the Spanish Commercial Code, the period is two years from the date of the collision. A note of protest must be made by the captain in the first port of arrival. Otherwise the action will be forfeited (Article 953 of the Commercial Code). The solution is the same wherever the 1910 Collision Convention applies (*cf.* Article 7 of the Convention).

Sweden

The time-bar period is two years from the date when the damage occurred as provided by the 1910 Collision Convention.

Switzerland

In accordance with the 1910 Collision Convention, Art. 7, the claims are time-barred after two years from the date of the incident (Article 121, section 1 of the Swiss Maritime Code).

Turkey

The prescription period is two years from the date of the collision (Article 1259/II, paragraph 2 and Article 1261 of the Commercial Code).

United Kingdom

The Maritime Conventions Act 1911 stipulates that an action in respect of collision for damages to property or cargo, personal injury, or loss to another vessel, or in respect of any salvage services, must be brought against the other vessel within two years. The two-year period commences to run from the date when the damage, loss or injury was caused or the salvage services were rendered. The competent court has discretion to extend the period if it is satisfied that there has not been any reasonable opportunity for the plaintiff to arrest the defendant vessel during the limitation period (Maritime Conventions Act 1991, s. 8)

United States

Collision is a maritime tort and laches[7] applies. The period commences to run from the date of the collision.[8]

Venezuela

Indemnity actions for collision damage are extinguished (*caducidade*):

(a) if the master fails to make and notify the note of protest within 24-hours from the moment on which he is able to file the protest, and

(b) if, having timely filed and notified the protest, no legal proceedings are commenced within 30 days from the date of notification (Commercial Code, Arts. 895 and 897).

The above provisions do not apply in cases where the collision has caused the total loss of the ship (Commercial Code, Art. 895) in which event the special five-year prescription period running from the day of the occurrence is probably applicable (Commercial Code, Art. 893).

2. POLLUTION

Uniform Rules

Article 8 of the International Convention on Civil Liability for Oil Pollution Damage of 1969 (CLC 1969) provides that rights of compensation under the Convention shall be extinguished unless action is brought within three years from the date when the damage occurred. The lapse of

7. See page 9 above.
8. Schoenbaum, note 5 at page 10, above, 74–80, 156.

time, as in the Hague Rules, does not merely affect the action, but causes the extinction of the right. It is worth noting that whilst in other conventions, such as the 1910 Collision and Salvage Conventions, the 1974 Athens Convention and the Hamburg Rules, the terms used are in English "time bar" or "limitation of action" and in French "prescription", in the CLC the term used is in both languages "extinction" as in the 1926 and in the 1967 International Conventions for the Unification of Certain Rules Relating to Maritime Liens and Mortgages (Maritime Liens and Mortgages Conventions).

Since the three-year limit commences to run from an event (the occurrence of the damage) which may not be known to the person liable, in order to avoid unlimited uncertainty Article 8 then provides for a maximum period of six years from the date of the incident which caused the damage. It is worth noting that the text differs from the previous one in that whilst in the former sentence it is provided that rights of compensation are extinguished unless action is brought, in the second sentence no reference is made to the effects of the failure to bring an action within the prescribed time limit, but it is merely provided that no action may be brought after six years.

However, the provision is necessarily linked to the first one and, therefore, the effect of the impossibility to bring an action is clearly that specified in the first sentence, namely the extinction of the right of compensation. Finally, Article 8 clarifies when the time commences to run where the incident which causes the damage consists of a series of occurrences; in such a case the time commences to run from the date of the first such occurrence.

Argentina

There is no time limit specifically indicated in the *Ley de Navegacìon* and, consequently, the period of prescription for actions for tort liability must be applied. This is two years from the date of the occurrence (Article 4037 of the Civil Code).

Australia

Claims for oil-pollution damage, although tort like, would be made under the Protection of the Sea (Civil Liability) Act 1981 (Cth).

Rights of action for oil-pollution damage are extinguished unless brought within three years from the date when the damage occurred, and in no case can an action be brought more than six years from the date of the incident which caused the damage: Protection of the Sea (Civil Liability) Act 1981 (Cth), Sch. 1, Art. VIII.

Belgium

The prescription period is three years from the date when the damage occurred (Law of 20 July 1976, incorporating the 1969 CLC).

Brazil

There is no special prescription period in respect of claims for pollution damage and, therefore, the general 20-year prescription period (Article 442 of the Commercial Code and Article 177 of the Civil Code) applies.

Canada

Section 677(10) of the Canada Shipping Act 1936 states:

> No action in respect of a matter referred to in subsection (1) (oil pollution damage caused by a ship and Public Authority measures taken to clean up or prevent pollution damage) lies unless it is commenced:
>
> (a) where pollution damage occurred, within three years after the day on which the pollution damage occurred, and within six years after the occurrence which caused the pollution damage; or
> (b) where no pollution damage occurred, within six years after the occurrence.

Chile

The prescription period is three years starting from the date the damage occurred or the preventive measures were taken. However, no action whatsoever may be brought after six years starting from the date of the incident. When the incident consists of a series of occurrences the six years period shall run from the date of the first such occurrence (Article 146, paragraph 5 of the Navigation Law).

China

The prescription period is three years. China is a party to the CLC 1969.

Article 261 of the Chinese Maritime Code (the Code was adopted on 7 November 1992 by the Standing Committee of the Seventh China People's Congress and will enter into force on 1 July 1993) provides that claims arising out of collision between vessels must be brought within two years from the date of the collision.

Croatia

Claims for damage resulting from oil pollution are time barred after three years from the date when the damage occurred (Article 849, paragraph 1 of the Maritime Law). Rights of compensation under the provisions of Article 840—848 of the Maritime Law are extinguished unless an action is brought within six years from the date of the incident which caused the damage (Article 849, paragraph 2 of the Maritime Law). When the incident consists of a series of occurrences, the six-year period runs from the date of the first such occurrence (Article 849, paragraph 3 of the Maritime Law).

Denmark

The time-bar period is three years from the day the damage was caused. However, not later than six years from the day on which the accident occurred which caused the damage (Section 292, subsection 1 of the Danish Merchant Shipping Act).

Finland

Following the enactment into Finnish law of the 1969 CLC the time limit is three years from the date when the damage occurred, but in no case can it exceed six years from the date of the incident.

France

In case of oil pollution, Article 1 of Law 26 May 1977 makes reference to the 1969 CLC in respect of the "conditions and limits" of the liability. The prescription period starts to run three years from the date when the damage occurred, but in no case can an action be brought after six years from the date of the incident which caused the damage (e.g. when a tank of a sunken tanker breaks up six years after sinking).

In case of pollution caused by other substances, the general prescription period applies, *viz.* 10 years from the date when the damage occurred. (Article 2270–1 of the Civil Code, as amended by Law 5 July 1985).

Germany

The time-bar period is that provided by the CLC 1969. Its legal nature is that of an *Ausschlussfrist*.[9]

Greece

1. Fines may be imposed by the competent administrative authorities. Such fines charged to the master, crew, pilot or shipowner constitute,

9. See page 2 above.

according to a certain view,[10] a kind of compensation from the State for the additional expenses involved, because of the failure of the persons concerned to meet their obligation to avoid pollution. According to another view, such penalties are fines of an administrative nature[11] that are imposed as a result of an extended responsibility of the aforesaid persons, *viz*. of the master under Article 40 of the Code of Private Maritime Law (CPML) and of the owner under Article 84 of the same code.

Since the obligation to pay the fine arises from a tortious act, the respective claim, under Article 937 of the Greek Civil Code concerning prescription of claims in tort, becomes time-barred after a period of five years from the time when the damage and the person liable to pay compensation became known.

2. Under Law 314/1976 concerning "ratification of the International Convention on Civil Liability for Oil Pollution Damage, signed at Brussels on 29 November 1969, and settlement of relevant matters" the said Convention entered into force on 27 September 1976. According to Article 8 of the said Convention the rights of compensation for pollution damage caused on the territory, including the territorial sea of a Contracting State, shall be extinguished, unless an action is brought within three years from the date when the damage occurred, provided that in no case shall an action be brought after six years from the date of the incident which caused the damage.

India

The applicable time limit is three years from the date of accrual of the cause of action.

Ireland

The Oil Pollution of the Sea (Civil Liability and Compensation) Act 1988 has been passed by the legislature but its operation has been suspended until a commencement order has been executed by the Minister for Marine. This has not yet taken place.

When it does come into operation, this Act will give effect to the International Convention on Civil Liability for Oil Pollution Damage 1969 and to the International Convention on the Establishment of an International Fund for Compensation for Oil Pollution Damage 1971.

10. Judgment Nos. 1050/73 and 1398/72 of the Court of First Instance of Piraeus, Epitheoresis Nautiliacou Dicaiou—E.P.N. vol. 2, p. 152; vol. 1, p. 145.

11. Court of Appeal of Athens, judgment Nos. 1732/1974 E.N.D., vol. 3, p. 119, and No. 4218/1973 E.N.D., vol. 1, p. 320.

In that event, the appropriate time bar will be three years from the date of occurrence, but no later than six years (section 12(5) of the Oil Pollution of the Sea (Civil Liability and Compensation) Act 1988).

Until such time as the Act becomes operable, a claim for oil pollution damage would be determined by the ordinary law of tort which provides that an action claiming damages for negligence, nuisance, or breach of duty, shall not be brought after the expiration of six years from the date on which the cause of action accrued (section 11(2)(a), Statute of Limitations 1957).

Italy

Rights of compensation enforceable against the owner of a tanker are extinguished within three years, in accordance with Article 8 of the 1969 CLC. Rights of compensation enforceable against any other person are extinguished within five years in accordance with Article 2947 of the Civil Code.

Japan

Claims against a shipowner as defined in the Compensation for Oil Pollution Damages Act for pollution damage as defined in the Act, s. 2 (the definitions are the same as those given in Article 1 of the 1969 CLC) are time-barred three years from the date on which the pollution damage occurs, but not later than six years from the day on which the incident occurs (section 10 of the Act).

Korea

The extinction period is three years from the date when the damage occurred, or six years from the date of the first accident which caused the damage (Article 11, Act of Compensation for Oil Pollution Damage).

Malta

Articles 1–9 of the 1969 CLC, as amended by the 1976 Protocol and Articles 1–15 of the 1971 Fund Convention, as amended by the 1976 Protocol have been incorporated into and are enforceable as part of, Maltese law by the Oil Pollution (Liability and Compensation) Act 1991 (Act XV of 1991).

Rights of compensation under the 1969 CLC are time-barred three years after the date of the occurrence, but not later than six years.

In respect of rights of compensation under the 1971 Fund Convention the action should be brought thereunder, or a notification made within three years from, the date when the damage occurred but no later than six years from the date of the incident which caused the damage. Moreover, the right of the owner or his guarantor to seek indemnification from the International Oil Pollution Compensation Fund, pursuant to Article 5, paragraph 1 of the Fund Convention, shall in no case be extinguished before the expiry of a period of six months as from the date on which the owner or his guarantor acquired knowledge of the bringing of an action against him under the 1969 CLC.

Mexico

The prescription period is two years from the date of the casualty (Article 1161 of the Codigo Civil Federal).

Netherlands

The extinction period for claims in respect of oil-pollution damage is three years, commencing from the day on which the damage occurred but this period will not exceed six years commencing from the day of the incident which caused the damage, as provided by Article 8 of the 1969 CLC. This Article has been incorporated in the Dutch Oil Tankers Liability Act (Wet aansprakelijkheid olietankschepen). Claims in respect of (oil) pollution not falling within the scope of the CLC or the Dutch Oil Tankers Liability Act are governed by the regulations applicable to collision (Civil Code, Art. 8:541).[12]

Where claims are brought against parties not falling within the scope of the regulations applicable to collision, the general time-bar period of five years for actions founded on tort applies. It commences from the day following the day on which the victim has become aware of both the damage and the person liable. In any case, the right of action becomes time-barred after a period of twenty years following the event which has caused the damage (Civil Code, Art. 3:310).

Norway

The time bar is three years from the date on which the damage or loss occurred or the expense was incurred, but never later than six years after the incident upon which the liability is based.

Poland

There are no specific provisions under Polish law regarding prescription periods in respect of such claims. However, Poland has ratified the 1969 CLC.

12. See page 5 above.

According to Article 333, section 1 of the Maritime Code 1961, the rules of this Convention are applied to the liability for oil pollution damage, including Article VIII providing for a prescription period of three years from the date when the damage occurred; and providing further that in no case can an action be brought after six years from the date of the incident which caused the damage.

Portugal

The prescription period of a claim for damages is three years from the date when the person who has suffered the loss becomes aware of his right. This rule also applies when the person liable and/or the actual extent of the damage is not known, but does not affect the ordinary prescription period, calculated from the date of the occurrence of the incident (Article 498, no. 1 of the Civil Code).

Russia

Russia is a party to the 1969 CLC and, therefore, when the Convention applies the time limits, they are those set out in Article VIII of the Convention.

In all other cases claims for oil pollution damage become time-barred after the general period of three years which starts to run from the day on which the right to claim accrued, i.e. from the day the person knew or should have known about the infringement of his right.

Spain

The prescription period is three years from the date when the damage occurred, when the 1969 CLC applies.

Otherwise the general one-year prescription for tort liability is applicable.

Sweden

The time-bar period is three years from the date of occurrence, but not later than six years (1969 CLC—London Limitation Convention 1976).

Switzerland

The time bar is governed by the CLC 1969. Pursuant to Article 8, the time is three years from the date of the damage, but not longer than six years after the occurrence took place. Its legal nature is that of an extinction period (*Verwirkungsfrist*).[13]

13. See page 8 above.

Turkey

According to the Environment Act the prescription period is one year with a maximum period of 10 years—see introductory statement at page 12 above. If the Commercial Code is applied to pollution cases, the period is one year (Article 1259, paragraph 1) with no maximum period.

United Kingdom

In respect of claims for damages caused by oil pollution from merchant ships, the Merchant Shipping (Oil Pollution) Act 1971 stipulates that an action must be brought no later than three years after the claim arose, or later than six years after the occurrence or first of the occurrences resulting in the discharge or escape by reason of which the liability was incurred (Merchant Shipping (Oil Pollution Act) 1971, s. 9).

United States

An action for damages under the Oil Pollution Act of 1990 must be brought within three years after the date on which the loss and the connection of the loss with the discharge in question are reasonably discoverable with the exercise of due care. An action for removal costs must be commenced within three years after the completion of the removal actions (33 U.S.C. 2717).

Venezuela

The ordinary 10-year prescription period applies. Time starts running from the date of the occurrence (Article 132 of the Commercial Code).

3. OTHER DAMAGE TO THE ENVIRONMENT

Argentina

As with pollution, the time limit is two years.

Australia

Tort claims for other damage to the environment would be subject to the limits at page 15 above. Claims under the Protection of the Sea (Civil Liability) Act 1981 (Cth) for other damage to the environment by oil pollution would be subject to the three-year period described at page 22 above.

Brazil

There is no special prescription period, therefore, the general twenty-year prescription period (Article 442 of the Commercial Code and Article 177 of the Civil Code) applies.

Canada

The normal laws of tort would apply in most instances. Prescription will vary from province to province between three years under the new civil law provisions in Quebec; two years in British Columbia and six years in most other common law provinces timed from the date of the occurrence. However, exceptions are found in various provisions of the Canadian Fisheries Act 1868, the Canadian Environmental Protection Act 1988 and the Ontario Environmental Protection Act 1971, which each provide for a two-year time limit for Government claims for recovery of the cost of measures taken to protect the environment. While, not necessarily, exclusively damage to the environment, the cost of wreck removal is declared under section 18(2) of the Canadian Navigable Waters Protection Act 1886 to be a debt due to Her Majesty and is thus not a prescribable claim.

Chile

The same rules as for pollution apply.[14]

China

The Maritime Code has no stipulations in this regard. Article 265 of the Maritime Code shall apply where damage to the environment is caused by oil pollution by a ship.[15] Where the damage to the environment is caused by other events, it is likely that Articles 135 and 137 of the General Principles of Civil Law should apply, in which case the time-bar period as provided therein is two years from the time when the infringement of a right is or should have been known.

Croatia

Claims for other damage to the environment are time-barred after three years from the date the person who suffers the damage acquires the knowledge of the damage and of the person who caused such damage (Article 376, paragraph 1 of the Law of Obligations 1978). Irrespective of this pro-

14. See page 23 above.
15. See page 23 above.

vision, the claim is time-barred after five years from the date the damage occurred (Article 376, paragraph 3 of the Law of Obligations 1978).

Denmark

The time-bar period is five years from the day when the claimant had the possibility of discovering and establishing the extent of the damage (section 1, subsections 1–5 and section 3 of the Danish Act on Time Limitations).

France

The prescription period is 10 years (Article 2270–1 of the Civil Code).

Germany

In Germany no damages can be claimed if a pure damage to the environment occurs. If a damage to the environment causes personal injury or damage to property the time-bar period is that provided by the CLC 1969. Its legal nature is that of an *Ausschlussfrist*.[16]

Greece

There is no special statutory provision concerning the prescription in respect of damage to the environment other than pollution and damage to third parties at sea or ashore. In cases where such damage is caused by an unlawful act, whether wilful or negligent, for example when a vessel strikes against a quay, etc., the claim is time-barred after the lapse of a period of five years from the time when the damage and the person responsible for payment of the compensation have become known to the claimant (Article 937, section 1 of the Civil Code).

India

The applicable time limit is three years from the date of accrual of the cause of action.

Ireland

A claim other than for oil pollution damage is determined by the ordinary law of tort, which provides that an action claiming damages for negligence, nuisance, or breach of duty shall not be brought after the expiration of six years from the date on which the cause of action accrued (section 11(2)(a) of the Statute of Limitations (1957).

16. See page 2 above.

Italy

The applicable prescription period is five years (Article 2947 of the Civil Code).

Japan

The time-bar period is three years from the day on which the injured party became aware of such damage and of the identity of the person who caused it, but not later than 20 years after the day on which such unlawful act was committed (Civil Code, s. 724).

Korea

The right to claim damages that have arisen from an unlawful act, is extinguished by prescription if not exercised within three years from the time when the injured party or his legal representative becomes aware of such damages and of the liable person (Article 766(1) of the Civil Code) or, in any event, after 10 years from the time when the unlawful act is committed (Article 766(2) of the Civil Code). This is a general rule applicable to tort claims unless otherwise expressly stated.

Malta

The general rule in respect of tort applies, i.e. tort claims arising from other damage to the environment are barred after the lapse of two years.

Mexico

The prescription period is two years from the date of the casualty (Article 1161 of the Codigo Civil Federal).

Netherlands

All damage caused by a vessel, regardless of whether a collision has occurred or not, is governed—except in the event that the Oil Tankers Liability Act is applicable—by the regulations applicable to collision (Civil Code Art. 8:541). Hence the time-bar period of two years applies. See page 20 above.

Where claims are brought against parties not falling within the scope of the regulations applicable to collision, the general time-bar period of five years for actions founded on tort applies. It commences from the day following the day on which the victim has become aware of both the damage and the person responsible. Also, in all cases the right of action becomes time-barred after the lapse of a period of 20 years following the event which caused the damage (Civil Code, Art. 3:310).

Norway

The time-bar period is three years from the day the plaintiff gains or ought to have gained knowledge of the damage and of the party liable. (Ten years if the damage is done by an offence. In any case, the claim might be brought during criminal proceedings in which the offender is convicted).

The Limitation Act which has been enacted by Parliament and came into operation 1 January 1980, contains, in addition to the three-year limit from the day the plaintiff gains knowledge of the damage and of the liable person, two new limits. The claim is time-barred no later than 10 years after the damage was done and not later than twenty years after the day on which the act which caused the damage was carried out.

The absolute limits of 10 and 20 years respectively, are still applicable. In 1988 an exception was made to the 20-year absolute time limit, with regard to personal injury in cases where the damage is caused as a consequence of business activities or the like, and where the responsible party, or someone he has vicarious liability for, knows or ought to have known that the business activity could be dangerous to life or health, provided the responsible party had or ought to have had this knowledge before he ceased the particular dangerous activity. This exception from the 20-year time limit is aimed at, for instance, asbestos cases. Apparently, the absolute 10-year time limit running from the time when the damage occurred will supersede the exception from the 20-year time limit. In other words: in asbestos cases the injured party must commence action within ten years from actually feeling symptoms from the asbestos infection. One can readily foresee difficulty in court cases applying these amended rules. Suffice it to say that the 1989 amendment intended to extend the possibilities for the injured parties in getting compensation from the responsible party.

There is also a further extension, namely that a claimant who has not been pursuing his claim because he lacked knowledge of his claim and/or the responsible party may, regardless of what is stated above, file a claim within one year from the date when he actually gained or ought to have gained such knowledge. This latter extension is, of course, only relevant if one assumes that either the 10-year or 20-year period has elapsed, and the claimant, only after the lapse of one of these periods, gained sufficient knowledge about the responsible party.

None of these extensions and exceptions are, of course, applied very frequently, because in most tort cases the claimant has precise knowledge about the tort feasor as well as his claim at a fairly early stage, so the three-year time limit commences to run. This is mentioned to emphasize that one should never forget under Norwegian law that the general time limit is three years, but that there are as aforesaid certain exceptions and extensions available to the claimant.

Portugal

The prescription period of a claim for damages is three years from the date when the person who has suffered the loss becomes aware of his right. This rule also applies when the person liable and/or the actual extent of the damage is not known, but does not affect the ordinary prescription period, calculated from the date of the occurrence of the incident (Article 498, no. 1 of the Civil Code).

Russia

Russia is a party to the 1969 CLC and, therefore, when the Convention applies the time limits are those set out in Article VIII of the Convention.

In all other cases claims for oil pollution damage become time-barred after the general period of three years which starts to run from the day on which the right to claim accrued, i.e. from the day the person knew or should have known about the infringement of his right.

Spain

The one-year period for tort liability applies.

Sweden

The general period of time bar is 10 years.

Turkey

The same law as that for pollution damage regulates this matter. Therefore, there is no difference from the pollution damage.[17]

United Kingdom

The time limit for actions in tort is six years from the date on which the cause of action accrued (Limitation Act 1980, s. 2). In cases of negligence (except personal injury cases), time begins to run when the damage occurs, irrespective of whether the damage is known to the victim. However, in cases involving latent damage, the period is as follows:

17. See page 29 above.

(i) six years from the date on which the cause of action accrued or
(ii) three years from the earliest date when the damage was discovered or was reasonably discoverable (Limitation Act 1980, s. 14A).

The above is, however, subject to a long stop of fifteen years i.e. no action can be brought after the expiration of fifteen years from the date on which the act of negligence occurred (Limitation Act 1980, s. 14B).

United States

If a suit is based on a state environmental damage statute, then the limitation period in that statute will apply. Otherwise, laches[18] will apply.

Venezuela

The ordinary ten-year prescription period applies. Time starts running from the date of the occurrence (Article 132 of the Commercial Code).

4. DAMAGE TO THIRD PARTIES AT SEA OR ASHORE

Argentina

As with pollution damage and other damage to the environment, the time limit for damage to third parties is two years.

Australia

1. For ships on international and interstate voyages:
   (a) For damage to property on another ship or for death or personal injury suffered on another ship, two years: Navigation Act 1912 (Cth), s. 396(1).
   (b) For damage to other property (e.g. property ashore) or for death of or personal injury to other persons (e.g. swimmers or persons on the ship against which the action is brought):
   —New South Wales, Queensland and Tasmania:
   For *in personam* personal injury actions, three years.[19]
   For *in personam* property damage claims, six years.[20]
   For *in rem* actions (personal injury or property damage), no limit.[21]

18. See page 9 above.
19. Limitation Act 1969 (NSW), s. 18A; Limitation of Actions Act 1974 (Qld), s. 11; Limitation Act 1974 (Tas), s. 5 (1).
20. (Limitation Act 1969 (NSW), s. 14(1)(b); Limitation of Actions Act 1974 (Qld), s. 10(1)(a); Limitation Act 1974 (Tas), s. 4(1)(a).
21. Limitation Act 1969 (NSW), s. 22(1); Limitation of Actions Act 1974 (Qld), s. 10(6)(a); Limitation Act 1974 (Tas), s. 1.8(1).

—Northern Territory:

For all *in personam* actions (personal injury or property damage), three years.[22]

For all *in rem* actions (personal injury or property damage), no limit.[23]

—South Australia:

For all personal injury actions (*in rem* or *in personam*) three years.[24]

For all property damage actions (*in rem* or *in personam*) six years.[25]

—Victoria:

For all actions, six years.[26]

—Western Australia:

For all *in personam* actions (personal injury and property damage) six years.[27]

For all *in rem* (personal injury and property damage) actions, no limit.

2. For ships on intrastate voyages:

(a) New South Wales and Tasmania:

—For damage to property on another ship or for death or personal injury suffered on another ship, two years.[28]

—For damage to other property (e.g. property ashore) or for death of or personal injury to other persons (e.g. swimmers or persons on the ship against which the action is brought):

—For *in personam* personal injury actions, three years.[29]

—For *in personam* property damage actions, six years.[30]

—For all *in rem* actions (personal injury or property damage), no limit.[31]

(b) Northern Territory:

—For damage to property on another ship or for death or personal injury suffered on another ship, two years.[32]

22. Limitation Act 1981 (NT), s. 12(1)(b).
23. Limitation Act 1981 (NT), s. 20(2).
24. Limitation of Actions Act 1936 (SA), s. 36(1)).
25. Limitation of Actions Act 1936 (SA), s. 35(c).
26. Limitation of Actions Act 1958 (Vic), s. 5(1)(a) and s. 5(1A).
27. Limitation Act 1935 (WA), s. 38(1)(c)(vi).
28. Limitation Act 1969 (NSW), s. 22(2); Limitation Act 1974 (Tas), s. 8(2).
29. Limitation Act 1969 (NSW), s. 18A; Limitation Act 1974 (Tas), s. 5(1).
30. Limitation Act 1969 (NSW), s. 14(1)(b); Limitation Act 1974 (Tas), s. 4(1)(a).
31. Limitation Act 1969 (NSW), s. 22(1); Limitation Act 1974 (Tas), s. 8(1).
32. Limitation Act 1981 (NT), s. 20(3).

—For damage to other property (e.g. property ashore) or for death of or personal injury to other persons (e.g. swimmers or persons on the ship against which the action is brought):

—For all *in personam* actions (personal injury or property damage), three years.[33]

—For all *in rem* actions (personal injury or property damage), no limit.[34]

(c) Queensland:

—For *in personam* personal injury actions, three years.[35]

—For *in personam* property damage actions, six years.[36]

—For all *in rem* actions (personal injury or property damage), no limit.[37]

(d) South Australia:

—For all personal injury actions (*in rem* or *in personam*), three years.[38]

—For all property damage actions (*in rem* or *in personam*), six years.[39]

(e) Victoria:

—For all actions, six years.[40]

(f) Western Australia:

—For all *in personam* actions (personal injury and property damage), six years.[41]

—For all *in rem* (personal injury and property damage) actions, no limit.

Brazil

The ordinary 20-year prescription period applies (Article 442 of the Commercial Code and Article 177 of the Civil Code).

Canada

The normal laws of tort would apply in most instances. Prescription will vary from province to province between three years under the new civil law provisions in Quebec; two years in British Columbia and six years in most other common law provinces timed from the date of the occurrence.

33. Limitation Act 1981 (NT), s. 12(1)(b).
34. Limitation Act 1981 (NT), s. 20(2).
35. Limitation of Actions Act 1974 (Qld), s. 11.
36. Limitation of Actions Act 1974 (Qld), s. 10(1)(a).
37. Limitation of Actions Act 1974 (Qld), s. 10(6)(a).
38. Limitation of Actions Act 1936 (SA), s. 36(1).
39. Limitation of Actions Act 1936 (SA), s. 35(c).
40. Limitation of Actions Act 1958 (Vic), ss. 5(1)(a) and 5(1A).
41. Limitation Act 1935 (WA), s. 38(1)(c)(vi).

However, exceptions are found in various provisions of the Canadian Fisheries Act 1868, the Canadian Environmental Protection Act 1988 and the Ontario Environmental Protection Act 1971, which each provide for a two-year time limit for Government claims for recovery of the cost of measures taken to protect the environment. While, not necessarily, exclusively damage to the environment, the cost of wreck removal is declared under section 18(2) of the Canadian Navigable Waters Protection Act 1886 to be a debt due to Her Majesty and is thus not a prescribable claim.

Chile

In the case of oil-pollution damage the periods indicated on page 32, above shall apply.

In the case of other damage two situations must be distinguished:

(a) If the damage is the consequence of a collision or stranding, the general two-year period from the occurrence of the event governs.
(b) In the case of death or personal injuries, the civil action is prescribed after four years (Article 1248 of the Commercial Code).

China

The Maritime Code has no special stipulations in this regard. Articles 135 and 137 and paragraph 1 of Article 136 of the General Principles of Civil Law should apply.

Claims for damage to property are time-barred at the end of two years from the time when infringement of a right is or should have been known. However, a People's Court does not provide protection 20 years after the date on which infringement of right arises. Where there are special circumstances, a People's Court may extend the time-bar period for a lawsuit.

Claims for personal injury are time-barred at the end of one year and the time when the period commences to run is established by the Supreme People's Court. Where the injury is obvious, the time-bar period for a lawsuit counts from the date of injury. Where the injury is not discovered at the time of the incident, but is diagnosed through examination afterwards and proved to be caused by infringement of a right, the time-bar period counts from the date on which the injury is diagnosed.

Croatia

Claims for damage to third parties are time-barred after three years from the date the person who suffers the damage acquires the knowledge of the damage and of the person who caused such damage (Article 376, paragraph 1 of the Law of Obligations 1978). Irrespective of this provision, the claim is time-barred after five years from the date the damage occurred (Article 376, paragraph 3 of the Law of Obligations 1978).

Denmark

The time-bar period is five years from the day the damage occurred (section 1, subsection 1, Rule 5 of the Danish Act on Time Limitations).

France

As a general rule the 10-year period of Article 2270—1 of the Civil Code applies. However, damage to third parties caused by collision is subject to the prescription period of two years, provided for in respect of collision by Articles 7 and 4–3 of Law 7 July 1967.

A special case is that of damage caused to State immovable property (e.g. the quay of a port). Pursuant to the doctrine of public domain the action is not subject to any time limit.

The question arises as to whether the prescription of the civil action is superseded by that of the penal action (three years) in the case of loss of life or personal injury caused by a collision. The Court of Appeal of Douai[42] replied in the negative, in line with a judgment of the Cour de Cassation,[43] and of a judgment rendered in an aviation case by the Chambre mixte of the Cour de Cassation.[44] In line with the opinion expressed by Rodière[45] it is now accepted that the special rule of Article 9 of law 6 July 1967 applies both to personal injuries and to property damage and excludes the general provisions of Article 1382 of the Civil Code, as well as Article 10 of the Penal Code.

Germany

The time-bar period (*Verjährungsfrist*)[46] is three years commencing from the time when the person who sustains the damage gains the knowledge of the damage and of the person liable; maximum period 30 years.

Greece

Claims of stevedores for loss of life or personal injury and claims for damage to installations, quays, etc., become time-barred, according to the

42. Judgment of 9 March 1990, DMF 1991 RJ, 42.
43. Judgment of 29 January 1974, DMF 1974, 281.
44. Judgment of 24 February 1978, Gaz. Pal. 1978, 331 with note of Rodière.
45. Traité de Droit Maritime, *Evénements de mer*, n. 85.
46. See page 2 above.

general statutory provisions on limitation of actions, after a period of five years from the time when the person who suffered such loss or damage obtained knowledge of the same and of the person liable to pay damages (Article 937 of the Civil Code).

Hong Kong

The time bar is six years from the date of the cause of action (Limitation Ordinance, 1965, s. 4(1)(a)).

India

The applicable time limit is three years, running from the day when the cause of action arises.

Ireland

An action claiming damages in respect of personal injury or loss of life, whether at sea or ashore shall not be brought after the expiration of three years from the date on which the cause of action accrued (section 11(2)(b) of the Statute of Limitations 1957). An action founded on tort whether committed at sea or ashore, not including a claim for damages in respect of personal injury or loss of life, shall not be brought after the expiration of six years from the date on which the cause of action accrued. Should a claim cover both damage to property and loss of life or personal injury, an action shall be time-barred if not brought within three years. (Section 11 of the Statute of Limitations 1957).

Italy

Article 488 of the Navigation Code provides that damage caused by a ship without physical contact, such as wash or other similar causes, is subject to the rules applicable to collision and, therefore, the two-year prescription period applies. In all other cases the five-year period applies.

Japan

The time-bar period is three years from the day on which the injured party became aware of such damage and of the identity of the person who caused it, but not later than 20 years after the day on which such unlawful act was committed (Civil Code, s. 724).

Korea

The right to claim damages that have arisen from an unlawful act, is extinguished by prescription if not exercised within three years from the time when the injured party or his legal representative becomes aware of such damages and of the liable person (Article 766(1) of the Civil Code) or, in any event, after 10 years from the time when the unlawful act is committed (Article 766(2) of the Civil Code). This is a general rule applicable to tort claims unless otherwise expressly stated.

Malta

The general rule on tort claims applies: the time bar is two years.

Netherlands

All damage caused by a vessel, regardless of whether a collision has occurred or not, is governed—except in the event that the Oil Tankers Liability Act is applicable—by the regulations applicable to collision (Civil Code, Art. 8:541). Hence the time-bar period of two years applies.[47]

Where claims are brought against parties not falling within the scope of the regulations applicable to collision, the general time-bar period of five years for actions founded on tort applies, commencing to run from the day following that on which the victim has become aware of both the damage and the person liable. In all cases the right of action becomes time-barred after the lapse of a period of 20 years following the event which has caused the damage (Civil Code, Art. 3:310).

Norway

The time-bar period is three years from the day the plaintiff gains or ought to have gained knowledge of the damage and of the party liable. (Ten years if the damage is done by an offence. In any case, the claim might be brought during criminal proceedings in which the offender is convicted).

For further information, see page 33 above.

Poland

There are no specific provisions under Polish law regarding prescription periods in respect of such claims. However, Poland has ratified the 1969 CLC.

According to Article 333, section 1 of the Maritime Code 1961, the rules of this Convention are applied to the liability for oil pollution damage, including Article VIII providing for a prescription period of three years from the date when the damage occurred; and providing further that in no case can an action be brought after six years from the date of the incident which caused the damage.

47. See page 19 above.

Russia

The general three-year time limit applies.

Spain

If the damage does not arise out of collision, the one-year period for tort liability applies.

The notion of collision resulting from Article 13 of the 1910 Collision Convention is very wide. Therefore, the two-year period applies to damage caused by a ship without physical contact, such as wash or other similar causes.

Sweden

The time-bar period is two years.

Switzerland

The common law rules relating to time bars for extra-contractual claims apply. These are found in the Code of Obligations, Art. 60, s. 1, which reads as follows:

> The claim for damages or reparations is barred by the statute of limitations after one year from the date when the damaged person has received knowledge of the damage and of the identity of the person who is liable, but, in any event, after 10 years from the date when the act causing the damage took place.

Turkey

The prescription period is one year with a maximum of 10 years (Article 60 of the Code of Obligations)—see introductory statement on page 12 above.

United Kingdom

The time limit for personal injury actions is three years from

(a) the date on which the cause of action accrued; or
(b) the date of knowledge (if later) of the person injured (Limitation Act 1980, s. 11(4)).

The "date of knowledge" is the date on which the plaintiff first had knowledge

(a) that the injury was significant;
(b) that the injury was attributable to the act of negligence, nuisance or breach of duty;

(a) of the defendant's identity;
(b) if the act was committed by a person other than the defendant, the identity of that person and the additional facts supporting the bringing of an action against the defendant (Limitation Act 1980, s. 14(1)).

Actions in tort for damage caused to property are subject to a limitation period of six years from the date on which the cause of action accrued (Limitation Act 1980, s. 2). See pages 34–35 above for cases concerning latent damage.

United States

If the Maritime Law applies to the cause of action, the statute of limitations is three years for personal injury and death claims by third parties, 46 U.S.C., 763a, and laches applies for damage done to property. If the maritime law does not apply, then the local state statutes of limitation apply.[48] The period commences to run from the date of the injury.

5. DAMAGE TO THE SALVED SHIP DURING SALVAGE OPERATIONS

Argentina

The time limit is two years in accordance with the period for tort liability commencing from the date of completion of the operations (Article 385 of the Ley de Navegacíon).

Australia

Where the action is in tort, the periods are as specified on page 15 above. If the damage to the salved ship forms part of an action for salvage reward, the periods are as on page 127 below.

Canada

The normal laws of tort would apply in most instances. Prescription will vary from province to province between three years under the new civil law provisions in Quebec; two years in British Columbia and six years in most other common law provinces timed from the date of the occurrence. However, exceptions are found in various provisions of the Canadian Fisheries Act 1868, the Canadian Environmental Protection Act 1988 and the Ontario Environmental Protection Act 1971, which each provide for a

48. Schoenbaum, see note 5 at page 10 above, 74–80.

two-year time limit for Government claims for recovery of the cost of measures taken to protect the environment. While, not necessarily, exclusively damage to the environment, the cost of wreck removal is declared under section 18(2) of the Canadian Navigable Waters Protection Act 1886 to be a debt due to Her Majesty and is thus not a prescribable claim. Section 471 of the Canada Shipping Act 1936 provides a two-year prescription period commencing at the time the salvage services have been completed.

Chile

Two years starting from the date of the incident whether the action is in contract or in tort (Article 1248 of the Commercial Code).

Croatia

Claims for damage to the salved ship are time-barred after three years from the date the person who suffers the damage acquires the knowledge of the damage and of the person who caused such damage (Article 376, paragraph 1 of the Law of Obligations 1978). Irrespective of this provision, the claim is time-barred after five years from the date the damage occurred (Article 376, paragraph 3 of the Law of Obligations 1978).

Denmark

Five years from the day the damage was incurred (section 1, subsection 1, Rule 5 of the Danish Act on Time Limitations).

France

In the absence of a special rule, the general provision of Article 2270–1 of the Civil Code (10 years) applies, such prescription being the same as that set out by Article 189 of the Code de Commerce.

A special problem may arise when the salved ship is damaged by the salvor in the course of the salvage operations carried out pursuant to a salvage contract. In the absence of an express provision in the 1910 Salvage Convention, to which reference must first be made, it is not certain that the 10-year prescription would be applied by French tribunals, since such prescription is provided only in respect of civil liability in tort.

Germany

The time-bar period (*Verjährungsfrist*) is three years commencing from the time when the person who sustains the damage gains the knowledge of the damage and of the person liable; maximum period 30 years.

Greece

The prescription period for damage to a salved ship during salvage operations depends on the cause of the damage. In cases where the cause of the damage is an unlawful act of the master, crew, pilot or shipowners of the salving ship, the general rule of Article 937, section 1 of the Civil Code applies. Pursuant to the above provision, claims in tort become time-barred after the lapse of a period of five years as of the time when the damage and the person liable to pay compensation become known.

However, where there is a contract for assistance or salvage, such a contract is usually defined as a contract for work, in which case the general rule of the 20-year prescription period (Article 249 of the Civil Code) normally applies. The period begins to run as of the time the claim arose and was actionable (Article 251 of the Civil Code).

Hong Kong

The time bar is six years from the cause of action (Limitation Ordinance 1965, s. 4(1)(a)).

Ireland

Any claim resulting from damage caused to a salved ship during salvage operations must be commenced within six years from the date when such damage was caused (section 11(2)(a) of the Statute of Limitations 1957), unless the damage has been caused by collision, in which case the period of limitation is two years (section 46 of the Civil Liability Act 1961).

Insofar as any such claim may also give rise to a contract claim, such claim is governed by section 11 of the Statute of Limitations 1957, which provides a time limit of six years from the date of the breach of contract.

Italy

The general five year period applies.

Japan

1. For claims against salvors for default in performance of the contractual obligations:

(i) In the case of both or either parties to the contract being "trader(s)" (Shonin) (a company is deemed a "trader" under Japanese law) who engages in commercial transactions as a business on his own behalf, the time limit is five years from the day on which the damage occurred (Commercial Code, s. 522)

(ii) In other cases, it is 10 years from the day on which the damage occurred (Civil Code, s. 167(1)).

2. For claims in tort, the time limit is three years from the day on which the injured party became aware of such damage and of the identity of the person who caused it, but no later than 20 years after the day on which such unlawful act was committed (Civil Code, s. 724).

Korea

The right to claim damages that have arisen from an unlawful act, is extinguished by prescription if not exercised within three years from the time when the injured party or his legal representative becomes aware of such damages and of the liable person (Article 766(1) of the Civil Code) or, in any event, after 10 years from the time when the unlawful act is committed (Article 766(2) of the Civil Code). This is a general rule applicable to tort claims unless otherwise expressly stated.

Malta

The general rule for tort claims applies. Claims for damage to the salved ship during salvage operations are barred after the lapse of two years. However, if damages can be related to a pre-existing contractual relationship, the general rule on claims arising out of contracts applies and such claims are barred after the lapse of five years. The applicable period of prescription is that of five years (Civil Code s. 2156(f)), unless the claim is based on a public deed, in which case the action would be barred after the lapse of 30 years.

Netherlands

The time-bar period is two years commencing to run from the day following the day on which the salvage operations are terminated (Civil Code, Article 8:1820).

Norway

The time-bar period is three years from the day the plaintiff gains or ought to have gained knowledge of the damage and of the party liable. (Ten years if the damage is done by an offence. In any case the claim might be brought during criminal proceedings in which the offender is convicted).

For further information, see page 33 above.

Portugal

The prescription period of a claim for damages is three years from the date when the person who has suffered the loss becomes aware of his right. This rule also applies when the person liable and/or the actual extent of the damage is not known, but does not affect the ordinary prescription period, calculated from the date of the occurrence of the incident (Article 498, no. 1 of the Civil Code).

Spain

There are no special rules. The general one-year period for actions in tort applies.

Sweden

If the damage occurs in connection with and due to the usage of another vessel the time limit will be two years (Collision Convention of 1910).

If, instead, e.g. a crane is used, the time bar will be the general time limit of 10 years.

Switzerland

The common law rules relating to time bars for extra-contractual claims apply. These are found in the Code of Obligations, Art. 60, s. 1.

Turkey

The prescription period is one year (Article 1259, paragraph 1 of the Commercial Code).

United Kingdom

If the damage was caused by a negligent act/omission, this can found an action in tort which has a limitation period of six years. If the damage gives rise to a claim in contract, the limitation period is six years from the date of the breach of contract (Limitation Act 1980, s. 5).

United States

This is a maritime claim and laches[49] applies. The period commences to run from the date the damage was done to the salved ship.[50]

49. See page 9 above.
50. Schoenbaum, see note 5 at page 10, 74–80, 101.

C. CONTRACT CLAIMS

Canada

Freedom of contract will allow the parties whatever provision they choose, so long as it is not contrary to public order. In the absence of specific provision, the prescription varies from province to province, but basically it is three years under the new civil law provision in Quebec and six years in most of the common law provinces from the date the claim/cause of action arose, although in British Columbia there is a two-year prescription period.

China

The general prescription period, which is applicable unless otherwise provided, is two years (Article 135 of the General Principles). Except as otherwise provided, the prescription period commences to run from the time when the infringement of the right is known or should have been known but no protection is afforded after the lapse of 20 years from the date of the infringement (Article 137 of the General Principles).

Germany

All time-bar periods in respect of contract claims have the legal nature of *Verjährungsfristen*,[1] except for claims in respect of loss of or damage to cargo, where there are two different time-bar periods. See page 85 below.

Israel

Under the Limitation Act, 1958 the time bar for all claims is seven years; however the Act does not apply to claims which are, by the relevant law of contract or by agreement, subject to the Hague Rules. Those claims become time barred according to the provisions contained in the Hague Rules. The limitation period starts from the accrual of the cause of action.

Italy

The ordinary prescription period is 10 years (Article 2946 of the Civil Code). However shorter periods are provided in respect of several contract claims and, in particular, in respect of all, or almost all, maritime claims in a strict sense.

1. See page 2 above.

Korea

The general rule, unless otherwise expressly stated, is that contract claims are extinguished after five years (prescription period) from the date when the claim accrued (Article 64 of the Commercial Code).

Malta

In commercial matters, the general rule is that the period specified by law for acquiring a prescription is shorter than that specified with respect to civil matters. Barring this difference between prescription in commercial matters and that in civil matters, all the other provisions of the law established in the Civil Code in respect of the latter apply to the former. Section 2156(f) of the Civil Code provides that actions for the payment of any debt arising from commercial transactions or causes, unless such debt is, under the civil or any other law, barred by the lapse of a shorter period or unless it results from a public deed, are barred by the lapse of five years.

Poland

The Maritime Code contains no general rules as to prescription periods of contract claims but some specific provisions.

Spain

The general prescription period for all personal actions, which is applicable unless otherwise provided, is fifteen years (Article 1964 of the Civil Code). Also as a general rule, the time begins to count as of the date when the action may be exercised (Article 1969 of the Civil Code). Once the liability is established by judgment, the action for the enforcement of the judgment commences to run from the date of such judgment (Article 1971 of the Civil Code).

However, much shorter periods are provided with respect to several contract claims. And this is particularly so with respect to the most common maritime claims.

Switzerland

The general rule for contractual claims is that there is a prescription period (*Verjährungsfrist*) of 10 years (Article 127 of the Code of Obligations). In many parts of the law special provisions regarding time bars are applicable whether based on special provisions of the Code of Obligations, the Maritime Code or the respective applicable Convention.

Turkey

All time-bar periods in respect of contract claims have the legal nature of a prescription period except for claims in respect of loss of, or damage to, cargo where the time-bar period has the legal nature of an extinction period.

United Kingdom

The time limit for actions founded in contract is six years from the date of the breach, unless the parties agree to reduce the period (Limitation Act 1980, s. 5).

If the parties agree to reduce the limitation period by contract the Unfair Contract Terms Act 1977 may apply. This Act provides that in certain circumstances (Unfair Contract Terms Act 1977, s. 3(1)) parties may not exclude or restrict liability unless such term satisfies the requirement of reasonableness, and that, in respect of claims for personal injury or death arising from negligence, liability cannot be excluded or restricted.

Schedule 1 of the Act provides that save for cases of personal injury and death, the provisions of the Act do not apply to contracts of marine salvage or towage, charterparties or contracts for the carriage of goods by ship or hovercraft except where a person is dealing as a consumer, and that contracts of insurance are not covered by the Act.

1. SHIPBUILDING AND SHIP REPAIRS

Argentina

An action against shipbuilders for construction and repairs is prescribed after a period of 10 years. This is the usual period for actions which have no special period assigned. Actions instituted against the shipbuilder for latent defects are prescribed at the end of one year from the date when the defects become known to the claimant (Art. 151 of the Ley de Navegacìon).

Belgium

The prescription period is 30 years (Article 2262 of the Civil Code) or a shorter period agreed upon by the parties.

Chile

The prescription period is two years starting from the delivery of the vessel, or from the date when the work should have been completed.

Croatia

Claims resulting from shipbuilding or repair contracts arising from latent defects that are discovered in the year after the construction or repair of the ship has been made, and that have been notified in writing to the shipbuilder or repairer, are time-barred after a period of one-year from the date of notification (Articles 432 and 433 of Maritime Law). For other claims arising from shipbuilding or repair contracts, the time-bar period of three years applies (Article 374 of the Law of Obligations 1978).

France

The action in respect of the warranty for latent defects of the new building or of the repaired ship is prescribed after one year from the discovery of the defect (Article 5 of Law 67–5 of 3 January 1967).

The action for non-conformity (which is often difficult to distinguish from that for latent defect) is subject to the general ten-years prescription period (Article 189 bis Code de Commerce, as amended by Law 3 January 1977). A recent judgment, rendered in respect of a defect of a mobile home but also relevant for a ship, excludes the application of the special prescription period provided for defects in respect of all defects "of a nature such as to create a danger to persons and to property".[2] However, in order to avoid the application of the short prescription period of the action *ex contractu* in respect of property it would be convenient to utilize the notion of "*faute dolosive*" (wilful negligence).

Germany

Claims against the shipowner for payment of money are extinguished after four years counted from the end of the year in which the payment becomes due. Claims against the shipyard for warranty of quality are extinguished after six months, commencing from the acceptance of the completed work.

Greece

1. Claims arising out of the performance of work relating to shipbuilding or repairs become time-barred after a period of one year (Article 289, section 3 of the Code of Private Maritime Law, hereinafter cited as CPML), beginning from the end of the year in which the time-bar period started to run (Article 291, section 1 of the CPML). According to Article 251 of the Civil Code, the prescription period begins to run as of the time at which the claim arose and was actionable.

2. Cour de Cassation, 1st Chambre Civile, 11 June 1991, Bulletin I, n. 201.

The ascertainment of this time raises certain issues. The CPML does not specify the "starting point" of the prescription. The problem becomes complex because according to Article 5 of the CPML, the provisions of Article 693 of the Civil Code (which provides for the "starting point" of the prescription) does not apply to shipbuilding contracts.

The correct view is that Article 5 of the CPML refers only to claims against shipbuilders in respect of deficiencies in ships when built and, therefore, the rest of Article 693 remains applicable. In accordance with the above view, the prescription periods begin to run from the end of the year in which the ship was received by the customer (Article 693 of the Civil Code). If, however, the shipbuilding contract provides that the liability of the shipbuilder for defects in the ship continues for a certain period from the date of the ship's delivery to the customer in case of doubt the limitation period regarding defects and deficiencies that have appeared within the said period will begin to run as of the time they were revealed.

2. Claims against shipbuilders in respect of deficiencies in ships when built become time-barred after a period of two years (Article 290, section 4 of the CPML) beginning from the end of the year within which the prescription period started to run (Article 291, section 1). According to Article 251 of the Civil Code, the prescription period begins to run as of the time when the claim arose and was actionable.

Hong Kong

Pursuant to section 4(1) of the Limitation Ordinance 1965, the time bar for all simple contracts is six years from the date of the cause of action.

Ireland

The time limit is six years from the date "the cause of action" arises.

Italy

Pursuant to Article 240 of the Navigation Code, claims against the builder in respect of defects of the ship are prescribed within two years of delivery. The customer who is sued for the payment of the price may however enforce the guarantee even after the lapse of two years, provided he has notified the defect within two years. This provision applies by analogy to shiprepair contracts. Other claims against the builder and shiprepairer and all claims by the latter against their customer, are subject to the ordinary ten-year prescription period.

Japan

For claims against a contractor by the person ordering the work for rectification of the defect existing in the subject matter of the work or compensation for damages, the time limit is one year from the day on which the subject matter of the work was delivered (Civil Code, s. 637(1)).

For claims of the contractor, in respect of a job, against the person ordering such work, the time limit is three years from the day of the completion of the work (Civil Code, s. 170(ii)).

Korea

The prescription period of claims for payment is three years from the date when the payment becomes due (Article 163(3) of the Civil Code).

The prescription period for claims due to defects against the shipbuilder is one year from the date of the delivery of the ship (Article 670(1) of the Civil Code).

Malta

Actions of builders of ships or other vessels, and of contractors in respect of construction or other works made of wood, steel or other material, for the works carried out by them or for the materials supplied by them, are barred by the lapse of two years (section 2149(a) of the Civil Code). Prescription takes place even though there may have been a continuation of supplies, deliveries on credit, labour services or other works. Nevertheless, in such case, where the claim in respect of such supplies, deliveries, labour, services or other work is evidenced by an approved account or other written declaration of the debtor, the action shall not be barred except by the lapse of five years to be reckoned from the date of such account or declaration (section 2151 of the Civil Code).

Mexico

The prescription period is one year from the date when the action can be brought (Article 1043 of the Commercial Code).

Netherlands

The time-bar period is five years commencing to run from the day following the day on which the claim has become exigible (Civil Code, Art. 3:307), unless a shorter period is provided for in the contract.

Norway

The general three-year time limit will apply. For contract claims of this nature, the period commences to run from maturity of the claim. If the maturity date is agreed in advance, there is no problem; otherwise the date of the default will at the same time constitute the maturity date for the compensation claim as a result of the default. If the default is accelerating a previously agreed maturity date, the three-year time limit commences to run only from the date the claimant notifies the debtor that he will invoke the default as an acceleration reason. If he fails to notify in this way, the original maturity date will constitute the commencement of the three-year time limit.

Portugal

Although there is no legal definition of a shipbuilding contract, the Commercial Code, Art. 489, in referring to the builder alternatively as the *construtor* (builder) or the *empreiteiro* (entrepreneur), seems to indicate that the builder can be qualified as an entrepreneur and thus the rules governing the contract for work and materials apply.

As respects such a contract, Article 1220 of the Civil Code provides that the customer must notify the contractor of the defects of the work within 30 days of their discovery, otherwise the rights granted to him by the subsequent articles are foreclosed.

Article 1224 of the Civil Code provides that the right to have the defect repaired, and to obtain a reduction of the price, the termination of the contract and payment of damages will be foreclosed if not enforced within one year from the moment of the refusal of acceptance of the work (or of its acceptance with reservations), without prejudice to the provisions of Article 1220. It further provides that if the defects were unknown at the time of acceptance of the work the one-year time limit commences to run from the time of discovery, but in no case can a claim be made after two years from the acceptance.

Finally, Article 1226 provides that any action for indemnity of the contractor against the subcontractors is foreclosed if the defects are not notified to the subcontractors within 30 days of their discovery.

Spain

Pursuant to Article 952 of the Commercial Code, the prescription period for actions arising out of work and services in relation to the construction or repairs of a ship, is one year from the date when the work was done and the services were rendered.

However, the jurisprudence, together with the majority of legal writers are of the view that the above article is not applicable to claims against the shipbuilder arising from defects of the construction. Instead it has been held that the general contractual period of 15 years applies.[3]

3. See judgment of the Tribunal Supremo of 18 February 1982 and Arroyo, I., in *Anuario de Derecho Maritimo*, V. III, pp. 385–404.

Sweden

The general period of time bar—10 years—is applicable.

Switzerland

For building and repair contracts of a vessel Article 371 of the Code of Obligations will apply, whereby all warranty actions for default are time barred after one year from delivery.

Turkey

The prescription period for claims against the shipyard (warranty of quality) is six months from the acceptance of the completed work, but this period can be extended (Articles 363 and 207 of the Code of Obligations; Article 25, paragraph 4 of the Commercial Code).

Claims against the shipowner for payment of money are prescribed five years after the date on which the payment becomes due (Article 126, paragraph 4 of the Code of Obligations).

United Kingdom

The time limit for a claim in contract is six years from the date of breach. If a party attempts to restrict or exclude liability, e.g. by reducing the time limit, the Unfair Contract Terms Act 1977 will apply only in circumstances where a party is dealing as a consumer or where the parties are dealing on standard terms (Unfair Contract Terms Act 1977, s. 3(1)).

United States

1. *Shipbuilding.* A shipbuilding contract is not a maritime contract, and, therefore, not within the federal admiralty jurisdiction.[4] Shipbuilding contracts are governed by the statutes of limitations of the different states for contract cases. The Uniform Commercial Code is in force and is applicable to shipbuilding contracts in all states except Louisiana and section 2–725 provides that suit must be brought within four years of the breach.

2. *Ship Repair Contracts.* These are maritime contracts and laches[5] applies. The period commences to run from the date of the breach of the contract.[6]

4. *People's Ferry Co.* v. *Beers*, 61 U.S. 393 (1857).
5. See page 9 above.
6. Schoenbaum, see note 5 at page 10 above, 99.

2. SUPPLIES TO SHIP

Argentina

There is no special period indicated as in the old Commercial Code. The prescription period for actions arising out of a contract is 10 years.

Belgium

The prescription period is one year after the date of supply (Article 270 of the Commercial Code, Book II).

Chile

The prescription period is two years starting from the date when the obligation falls due (Article 1248 of the Commercial Code).

Croatia

The time-bar period is three years from the day of each supply (Article 374 of the Law of Obligations 1978).

Finland

The general 10-year time limit applies.

France

The prescription period is one year from the supply (Article 433 of the Code de Commerce, Law of 3 January 1977).

Germany

The time limit in respect of claims for payment is four years. The time limit in respect of claims for warranty of quality is six months.

Greece

Claims arising out of the supply of materials or victuals to a ship become time barred after a period of one year (Article 289, section 3 of the CPML) beginning from the end of the year in which the time-bar period started to run (Article 291, section 1 of the CPML). According to Article 251 of the Civil Code, the time-bar period begins to run when the claim arises and is actionable.

Hong Kong

Pursuant to section 4(1)(a) of the Limitation Ordinance 1965, the time bar for all simple contracts is six years from the date of the cause of action.

Ireland

The time limit is six years from the date on which the cause of action accrued.

Italy

Contracts for the supply of provisions, materials, etc. are ordinarily qualified as contracts of sale and, therefore, are subject to the provisions applicable to such contracts. Italy is a party to the U.N. Convention on Contracts for the International Sale of Goods of 1980 and, therefore, when the Convention applies pursuant to its Article 1, the time limit for an action of the buyer on account of the lack of conformity of the goods is two years, under Article 39(2) of the Convention. When Italian domestic law applies notice of nonconformity must be given within eight days from delivery and the prescription period is one year from delivery (Article 1495 of the Civil Code). As respects any other claim arising out of a contract of sale the ordinary ten years prescription period applies.

Japan

The time limit in respect of claims of the supplier against the purchaser for the payment of the supplies is two years from the day on which the claims accrued and became due (Civil Code, s. 173(i)).

Korea

The prescription period is three years (Art. 163(3) of the Civil Code).

Malta

Actions for the payment of timber and other things necessary for the construction, equipment and provisions of a ship, are prescribed after two years from the date on which such timber or other things have been supplied (section 544(c) of the Commercial Code). Actions for the payment of victuals supplied to seamen by order of the master are prescribed after one year from the day of such supply (section 544(b) of the Commercial Code). With regard to actions on other supplies to the ship, the general rule in respect of contract claims is applicable—the period is of five years.

Mexico

The prescription period is one year from the date when the action can be brought (Article 1043 of the Commercial Code).

Netherlands

The time limit is five years commencing to run from the day following the day on which the claim has become exigible (Civil Code, Art. 3:307), unless a shorter period is provided for in the contract.

When the U.N. Convention on the Sale of Goods of 1980 (to which the Netherlands are a party) is applicable, the time limit for the buyer to give the seller notice of a lack of conformity of the goods is, pursuant to Article 39 of the Convention, at the most two years.

Norway

The general three-year time limit will apply. For contract claims of this nature, the period commences to run from maturity of the claim. If the maturity date is agreed in advance, there is no problem; otherwise the date of the default will at the same time constitute the maturity date for the compensation claim as a result of the default. If the default is accelerating a previously agreed maturity date, the three-year time limit commences to run only from the date the claimant notifies the debtor that he will invoke the default as an acceleration reason. If he fails to notify in this way, the original maturity date will constitute the commencement of the three-year time limit.

Portugal

The same rules as for shipbuilding contracts apply. See page 54 above.

Spain

Article 952 of the Commercial Code applies and the prescription period is one year from the date when the supplies were made.

Sweden

The general period of time bar—10 years—is applicable.

Switzerland

Depending on the nature of the supply claims will be time barred after a prescription period of 10 years (Article 127 of the Code of Obligations) or of five years (Article 128 of the Code of Obligations).

Warranty claims of the ship towards the supplier are governed by the law on sales and, therefore, will be time barred after a one-year period as provided for by Article 60 of the Code of Obligations.

Turkey

The prescription period for claims against the supplier for warranty of quality is six months from the receipt of the supplies, but this period can be extended (Articles 363 and 207 of the Code of Obligations; Article 25, paragraph 4 of the Commercial Code).

Claims for payment of money are prescribed five years after the date on which the payment becomes due (Article 126, paragraph 4 of the Code of Obligations).

United Kingdom

The same principles applicable to shipbuilding and ship repairs apply here.

The time limit for a claim in contract is six years from the date of breach. If a party attempts to restrict or exclude liability, e.g. by reducing the time limit, the Unfair Contract Terms Act 1977 will apply only in circumstances where a party is dealing as a consumer or where the parties are dealing on standard terms (Unfair Contract Terms Act 1977, s. 3(1)).

The Unfair Contract Terms Act 1977 does not apply to international supply contracts (Unfair Contract Terms Act 1977, s. 26).

United States

These are maritime contracts and laches applies.[7] The period commences to run from the date of the breach of the contract.[8]

3. AGENCY AGREEMENTS

Argentina

There is no special prescription period indicated in the old Commercial Code for actions arising from agency agreements and therefore the period is 10 years.

Chile

The prescription period is two years starting from the date when the obligation falls due (Article 1248 of the Commercial Code).

7. See page 9 above.
8. Schoenbaum, see note 5 at page 10 above, 99, 156.

Croatia

The time-bar period is three years from the day of each supply (Article 374 of the Law of Obligations 1978). The time-bar period runs from the day when each service was rendered.

Finland

The general 10-year time limit applies.

France

The prescription period is one year in respect of actions of the shipowner against the maritime agent (*consignataire de navire*: Article 16 of Law 3 January 1969); the general prescription period (10-years: Article 433 of the Code de Commerce) applies instead to the actions of the agent against the shipowner.

The one-year prescription period applies to actions of the consignee against the maritime agent of the consignee (*consignataire de la cargaison*: Article 16 of Law 3 January 1969), whilst the general 10-year prescription period applies in all other cases (action of the *consignataire* against the consignee; action of the shipper against his agent).

Germany

The time limit is four years.

Greece

Claims of carrier's agents for monies and disbursements incurred in the performance of the agency agreement become time-barred after a period of five years (Article 250, section 5 of the Civil Code), which begins to run as of the time when the claim arose and was actionable (Article 251 of the Civil Code).[9]

Claims of the carriers against their agents for non-performance or inadequate performance of their contractual obligations become time-barred after a period of 20 years (Article 249 of the Civil Code), which begins to run from the time when the claim arises and is actionable (Article 251 of the Civil Code).

Hong Kong

Pursuant to section 4(1)(a) of the Limitation Ordinance 1965, the time bar for all simple contracts is six years from the date of the cause of action.

9. See Multi-Member Court of Piraeus, Decision Nos. 1004/78 and 2492/78.

Ireland

The time limit is six years from the date on which the cause of action accrued.

Italy

The ordinary 10-year prescription period applies.

Japan

For claims of an agent against the principal, and vice versa, both of or either of whom are (is a) "trader(s)" (*Shonin*), the time limit is five years from the day on which the claims accrued and became due (Commercial Code, s. 522).

Korea

The prescription period is five years (Article 64 of the Commercial Code).

Malta

The general time limit for contract claims is applicable: five years.

Netherlands

The time-bar period is five years commencing to run from the day following the day on which the claim has become exigible (Civil Code, Art. 3:307) unless a shorter period is provided for in the contract.

Norway

The general three-year time limit will apply. For contract claims of this nature, the period commences to run from maturity of the claim. If the maturity date is agreed in advance, there is no problem; otherwise the date of the default will at the same time constitute the maturity date for the compensation claim as a result of the default. If the default is accelerating a previously agreed maturity date, the three-year time limit commences to run only from the date the claimant notifies the debtor that he will invoke the default as an acceleration reason. If he fails to notify in this way, the original maturity date will constitute the commencement of the three-year time limit.

Poland

Claims under an agency contract are prescribed at the expiration of two years from the day when they fall due (Article 203 of the Maritime Code).

Portugal

The same rules as for shipbuilding contracts apply. See page 54, above.

Spain

Law number 12 of 27 May 1992 on contracts of agency applies also to ship agency. The ship agents who have increased with their work the number of clients or the volume of operations of the shipowner have a special right of compensation in case of extinction of the contract (see Article 28 of the law on agency). The agent also has a right of compensation in case the shipowner unilaterally terminates the contract (Article 29). In these two cases, the action of the agent is prescribed after one year from the time when the contract was extinguished.

For all other matters relating to prescription, Article 4 refers to the Commercial Code. As a result of most of the payments made by the agent being included in the disbursement account, Article 952 of the Commercial Code shall apply and thus the prescription period shall be one year from the moment the respective services were rendered.

As far as the services rendered by the agent which cannot be included in Article 952 of the Commercial Code, the prescription is the general one provided for agents in Article 1967.1 of the Commercial Code, i.e. three years.

Sweden

The general period of time bar—10 years—is applicable.

Switzerland

The general rule for contractual claims applies: the prescription period is 10 years.

Turkey

The prescription period is five years from the date on which the claim becomes due (Article 126, paragraph 4, of the Code of Obligations).

United Kingdom

The time limit is six years from the date of the breach.

If a party attempts to restrict or exclude liability, e.g. by reducing the time limit, the Unfair Contract Terms Act 1977 will apply only in circumstances where a party is dealing as a consumer or where the parties are dealing on standard terms (Unfair Contract Terms Act 1977, s. 3(1)).

An agent may rely upon a clause in the contract between his principal and the third party limiting liability if it can be demonstrated that it was intended that it should apply to him.[10] An action by the principal for an account must be brought within the time limit applicable to the claim which is the basis of the duty to account (Limitation Act 1980, s. 23).

United States

If the functions of the agent are maritime in nature, then laches[11] applies and the period commences to run from the date of the breach. If the functions of the agent are not maritime in nature, then the local state statute of limitations for contract actions applies.[12]

4. TERMINAL OPERATIONS (LOADING, STOWAGE, UNLOADING, STORAGE, ETC.).

Uniform Rules

The United Nations Convention on the Liability of Operators of Transport Terminals in International Trade (not yet in force) provides in its Article 12 paragraph 1 that any action under the Convention is time-barred if judicial proceedings are not instituted within a period of two years.

The rule on the commencement of the limitation period is based on that of the Hamburg Rules but regulates specifically the case where the goods are not received by the person entitled to their delivery. Article 12 paragraph 2(a) provides, in fact, that the limitation period commences "on the day the operator hands over the goods or part thereof to, or places them at the disposal of, a person entitled to take delivery of them". This Article, however, does not specify in which circumstances the goods may be deemed to have been placed at the disposal of the person entitled and, therefore, some uncertainty may exist, when the person entitled does not directly take delivery of the goods, as to the commencement of the

10. *The Eurymedon* [1975] A.C. 154.
11. See page 9 above.
12. Schoenbaum, see note 5 at page 10 above, 103.

limitation period. It is worth noting that the same alternative as to the commencement of the time bar does not exist in respect of the notice of loss or damage. In fact, pursuant to Article 11, such notice must be given "not later than the third working day after the day when the goods were handed over by the operator to the person entitled to take delivery of them, failing which the handing over shall be prima facie evidence of the goods being in the same conditions as described in the document issued by the operator".

In case of total loss the limitation period commences to run, pursuant to Article 12 paragraph 2(b), on the day the person entitled to make a claim receives notice from the operator that the goods are lost, or on the day that person may treat the goods as lost, whichever is earlier. According to Article 5 paragraph 4 the person entitled to receive the goods may treat them as lost if the operator fails to hand over the goods to or place them at the disposal of the person entitled to take delivery of them within 30 days after the date agreed or, failing any agreement, within 30 days after receiving a request for delivery.

Whilst in case the goods are handed over, reference is made to the person entitled to receive them, in case of total loss reference is made to the person entitled to make a claim.

The limitation period, as in the Hague-Visby Rules and in the Hamburg Rules, may be extended by the operator after it has commenced to run.

Article 12 paragraph 5 regulates the recourse action by the carrier (or another person) against the operator and not the recourse action by the operator. Paragraph 5 provides that such recourse action may be instituted after the two year limitation period provided for the action against the operator:

> . . . if it is instituted within 90 days after the carrier or other person has been held liable in an action against himself or has settled the claim upon which such action was based and if, within a reasonable period of time after the filing of a claim against a carrier or other person that may result in a recourse action against the operator, notice of the filing of such claim has been given to the operator.

There may not be any conflict between this provision and those on recourse actions in the Hague-Visby Rules and in the Hamburg Rules because under the relevant provisions of these two Conventions (Article 3 paragraph 6 *bis* and Article 20 paragraph 5 respectively) the action for indemnity may be instituted within the time allowed by the law of the State where proceedings are instituted and, if the Convention on Transport Terminal Operators is in force, such time is that set out in its Article 12.

Pursuant to Article 12 there are two conditions, namely that the action is instituted within 90 days and within a reasonable period after the filing of a claim that may result in a recourse action. Moreover, the settlement of a claim is relevant only if made after an action has been instituted.

Argentina

There is no specific prescription period for actions arising from contracts related to terminal operations.

In case any such action is deemed to be connected with a contract of carriage or of affreightment, the prescription period is one year as this is the time limit fixed for this type of contract (Articles 258 and 293 of the Ley de Navegacìon).

If the action is considered to be independent of the contract of affreightment, the prescription period is 10 years.

The prescription period corresponding to actions arising out of a deposit contract is also 10 years.

Australia

Any limitation period provided for in the contract would be regarded as valid. In the absence of such provision, the following limitation periods apply.

For *in personam* actions:

—New South Wales, Queensland, South Australia, Western Australia, Tasmania, Victoria:
Six years[13]

—Northern Territory:
Three years.[14]

For *in rem* actions:

—New South Wales, Queensland, Western Australia, Tasmania and Northern Territory:
No limit.[15]

—Victoria and South Australia:
Six years.[16]

Chile

The prescription period is two years starting from the date when the obligation falls due (Article 1248 of the Commercial Code).

13. Limitation Act 1969 (NSW), s. 14(1)(a); Limitation of Actions Act 1974 (Qld), s. 10 (1)(a); Limitation of Actions Act (1936) (SA), 1.35(a); Limitation Act 1935 (WA), s. 38(1)(c)(15); Limitation Act 1974 (Tas), s. 4(1)(a); Limitation of Actions Act 1958 (Vic), s. 5(1)(a).

14. Limitation Act 1981 (NT), s. 12(1)(a).

15. Limitation Act 1969 (NSW), s. 22(1); Limitation of Actions Act 1974 (Qld), s. 10(6)(a); Limitation of Actions Act 1935 (WA), s. 38; Limitation Act 1974 (Tas), s. 8(1); Limitation Act 1981 (NT), s. 20(2).

16. Limitation of Actions Act 1958 (Vic), s. 5(1)(a); Limitation of Actions Act 1936 (SA), s. 35(a).

Croatia

The time-bar period is three years from the day of each supply (Article 374 of the Law of Obligations 1978). The time-bar period runs from the day when each service was rendered.

France

A distinction must be drawn between the following cases:

(a) Actions for damage caused by loading, stowing, unstowing and unloading are prescribed after one year, from the time when the goods have been handed over or placed at the disposal of the consignee, or from the time when they ought to have been handed over, both in case such actions are brought against the carrier or against the stevedoring company (Law of 18 June 1966, Articles 32 and 56).

(b) Actions for damage caused by the storage of the goods are equally prescribed in one year, if they are brought against the carrier, the stevedoring company, the ships agent or the agent of the consignee.[17]

(c) Actions for damage caused by storage are subject to the general 10-year prescription period when they are brought against a non-maritime enterprise (private or public warehouse, surveyors etc.).

Germany

The time limit for actions for payment is four years. The time limit for actions for warranty of quality is six months.

Greece

There is no special provision concerning the limitation of actions in respect of terminal operations.

Hong Kong

Pursuant to section 4(1)(a) of the Limitation Ordinance 1965, the time bar for all simple contracts is six years from the date of the cause of action.

17. Articles 32 and 56 of Law, 18 June 1966, referred to above for carriers and stevedoring companies; Articles 13 and 15 of, Law, 3 January 1969 for ship's agents or agents of the consignee.

Ireland

Such claims are governed by the six-year limitation period appropriate to claims arising out of breach of contract (Statute of Limitations 1957, s. 11).

Italy

Terminal operations have the legal nature of contracts for work[18] and, therefore, are subject to the prescription period for such a contract which is the ordinary 10-year period (Article 2946 of the Civil Code). However it has been held[19] that claims for defective performance are subject to the two-year prescription period set out for contracts for work by Article 1667 of the Civil Code and that the claimant must, under penalty of forfeiture of his claim, give notice thereof to the terminal operator within 60 days, as provided for in Article 1667 of the Civil Code.

Japan

1. For claims against a warehouse operator who makes it his business to keep goods in custody in a warehouse for other persons:

(a) In a case where there is no bad faith on the part of the warehouse operator:

(i) claims for liability of a warehouse operator are extinguished when the depositor or the holder of the deposit receipt has taken delivery of the goods without any reservation and has paid the charges for storage and other expenses; provided, however, that this rule shall not apply if, in the event that there was damage or partial loss which was not immediately discoverable, the depositor or the holder of the deposit receipt has dispatched notice thereof to the warehouse operator within two weeks of the date of delivery (Commercial Code, ss. 625 and 588) and, further,

(ii) claims for loss of or damage to the goods deposited are extinguished upon the lapse of one year from the day on which such goods were taken out of the warehouse. In the event of a total loss of the goods deposited, these periods commence from the day on which the warehouse operator dispatched notice of such loss to the holder of the deposit

18. Court of Cassation 20 July 1962, no. 1960, *S.p.A. Henry Coe & Clerici* v. *Anglo Elementar and Others*, 1963 Dir. Mar., 67.

19. Court of Appeal of Trieste, 19 June 1959, *S.p.A. Henry Coe & Clerici* v. *S.p.A. Anglo Elementar*, 1960 Dir. Mar., 437.

receipt, or if such holder is unknown to him, to the depositor (Commercial Code, s. 626).

(b) In other cases, the claims are extinguished upon the lapse of five years from the day on which such claims accrued and became due (Commercial Code, s. 522).

2. For other claims from a customer against the contractor, and vice versa:

(a) In a case where both of, or either of, them is (are) a "trader(s)" (*Shonin*), claims are extinguished after five years from the day on which the claims accrued and became due (Commercial Code, s. 522).

(b) In other cases claims are extinguished after 10 years from the day on which the claims accrued and became due (Civil Code, s. 167(1)).

Korea

The prescription period is five years (Article 64 of the Commercial Code).

Malta

The Maltese Maritime Authority has the function inter alia to provide, maintain and operate ports in Malta and to provide, maintain and operate therein and in the approaches thereto adequate and efficient services and facilities[20] as it may from time to time consider necessary or advantageous for the proper, safe and efficient functioning of such ports, or as the Authority may otherwise deem it proper to provide in the public interest (sections 6(1)(a) and 8(3) of the Maltese Maritime Authority Act 1991).

Notwithstanding the provisions of any other law, no actions shall lie against the Authority or a contractor in relation to their responsibilities under the Maltese Maritime Authority Act 1991, or for any loss or damage caused to any person, vessel, goods, vehicles or other things whatsoever on board a ship unless:

(a) a claim in writing, giving such particulars as may reasonably be necessary, is given to the Authority or the contractor, as the case may be, not later than six months after the date on which the goods were accepted by the Authority or the contractor;

20. "Port facilities" is defined as meaning facilities for berthing, towing, mooring or moving of ships within a port or the approaches thereto, or in entering or leaving such port or approaches, for the loading and unloading of goods, or embarking or disembarking passengers to or from any such ship, or for the lighterage, sorting, weighing, warehousing or handling of goods, and for the carriage of passengers or goods in connection with such facilities.

(b) the action is commenced within 12 months from the date aforesaid.

The Authority or the contractor may extend the period specified in paragraph (a) above by such further period not exceeding six months as it may deem fit if it is satisfied that the claim could not reasonably have been made within the period specified as aforesaid. The Authority or the contractor shall not be liable beyond such limits or amounts established by law or in such circumstances as may be prescribed (section 65).

Mexico

The time limit for claims of stevedores is two years from the date of the casualty (Article 519.1 of the Ley Federal del Trabajo).

Netherlands

The time-bar period is five years, commencing to run from the day following the day on which the claim has become exigible (Civil Code, Art. 3:307), unless a shorter period is provided for in the contract.

Norway

The general three-year time limit will apply. For contract claims of this nature, the period commences to run from maturity of the claim. If the maturity date is agreed in advance, there is no problem; otherwise the date of the default will at the same time constitute the maturity date for the compensation claim as a result of the default. If the default is accelerating a previously agreed maturity date, the three-year time limit commences to run only from the date the claimant notifies the debtor that he will invoke the default as an acceleration reason. If he fails to notify in this way, the original maturity date will constitute the commencement of the three-year time limit.

Portugal

The same rules as for shipbuilding contracts apply. See page 54, above.

Spain

If the shipowner has a long-term contractual relationship with the terminal operator, the rules of Articles 28 and 29 of the law on agency may apply to the terminal operations (i.e. the terminal operator shall be treated as an agent).

Otherwise it seems difficult that operations such as loading, unloading, stowage, storage, etc. be included in Article 952 of the Commercial Code.

Therefore, the prescription should be three years as provided for "agents" (*here latu sensu*) in Article 1967(1) of the Commercial Code.

Sweden

The general period of time bar—10 years—is applicable.

Switzerland

Terminal operation contracts are not specifically dealt with in the Swiss Code of Obligations or the Maritime Code. They will therefore be treated as mandate since under Swiss law the mandate is seen as the basic service contract.

The prescription period under the law of mandate is governed by the general time-bar provisions of the Swiss Code of Obligations (10 years).

Turkey

Terminal operations have the legal nature of contracts of work. Therefore claims in respect of warranty of quality against the terminal operator are subject to a six-month prescription period (Code of Obligations, Arts. 363 and 207; Commercial Code, Art. 25, paragraph 4).

Claims against the carrier or the shipper are prescribed five years after the date on which the payment becomes due (Article 126, paragraph 4 of the Code of Obligations).

United Kingdom

As in other simple contract claims, the time limit is six years from the date of breach. The relevant provisions of the Unfair Contract Terms Act 1977 may apply in relation to restriction of liability. It has been held that a stevedore may have the benefit of the Hague-Visby one-year time limit if sued direct by the shipper.

United States

Loading, stowage, unstowage, unloading, and stevedoring contracts are all maritime and laches[21] applies. The period commences to run from the date of the breach of the contract. Storage contracts are generally not con-

21. See page 9 above.

sidered maritime and the local state statute of limitations for contract actions applies.[22]

5. CONTRACTS OF AFFREIGHTMENT (DEMISE CHARTERS, TIME CHARTERS, VOYAGE CHARTERS, TONNAGE AGREEMENTS, CARRIAGE OF CARGO IN A GENERAL SHIP) EXCEPT LOSS OF OR DAMAGE TO CARGO

Argentina

The prescription period for the action arising from the contract of affreightment is one year from date of termination of the voyage or from the date when the contract was cancelled (Article 258 of the Ley de Navegacìon).

Australia

For breach of a contract for outward-bound international carriage or carriage between Australian States evidenced in a bill of lading: one year from the time of discharge, or from when discharge should have occurred (Carriage of Goods by Sea Act 1991 (Cth), Sch, Art. 3, R. 6).

For breach of other contracts of affreightment: Any limitation period provided for in the contract would be regarded as valid. In the absence of such provision, the limitation periods set out in respect of terminal operations apply (see page 65 above).

Belgium

The general prescription period is three years from the date the voyage has been completed (Article 269 of the Commercial Code Book II). The prescription period for claims in respect of freight is one year from the date the voyage has been completed (Article 270 of the Commercial Code Book II).

Brazil

The prescription period is one year. Time runs, in respect of claims for freight and demurrage, from the date of delivery of the cargo (Article 449.3 of the Commercial Code).

22. Schoenbaum, see note 5 at page 10 above, 100–102.

Chile

The applicable prescription period is two years. The provisions of the Commercial Code, Article 1249 relating to the time when the prescription period commences to run differ in the various types of contract and are the following:

(a) with respect to bareboat charterparties and time charter-parties, the time commences to run from the date when the contract expires or its performance is definitely interrupted.

(b) with respect to voyage charterparties and tonnage agreements the time commences to run from the date of the expected completion of the contract or from the date of its termination or rescission. For the carriage of goods in a general ship the time commences to run from the date of delivery of the goods or a part thereof or from the date when the goods should be delivered.

China

The Maritime Code provides in Article 259 that claims regarding bareboat and time charterparties are time-barred at the end of two years, counting from the date on which the breach is or should have been known. Claims regarding voyage charterparties are time-barred at the end of two years, counting from the date on which the breach is or should have been known (Article 257, paragraph 2).

Croatia

All claims under contracts of affreightment in respect of the breach of contractual obligations (such as payment of freight, demurrage and dispatch), except loss of or damage to the cargo, are time-barred after one year (Article 679, paragraph 1 of the Maritime Law) running from the date the obligation should have been fulfilled (Article 679, paragraph 5, point 1 of the Maritime Law).

In respect of claims arising out of bareboat charterparties the time-bar period runs from the day the contract has been terminated, except claims for hire for which the time-bar period runs from the date the hire was due (Article 679, paragraph 5, point 5 of the Maritime Law).

In respect of claims arising out of towage contracts the time-bar period runs from the date the towage ended, except claims for hire for which the time-bar period runs from the date the towage remuneration was due (Article 679, paragraph 5, point 4 of the Maritime Law).

After a claim has arisen, the parties may agree in writing to extend the time-bar period (Article 679, paragraph 3 of the Maritime Law).

Finland

The general 10-year time limit applies.

France

All actions arising out of contracts of affreightment other than those in respect of damage to cargo (failure of the ship to arrive, delays, payment of freight, demurrage, damage to the ship) are prescribed after one year (Article 4 of Law 18 June 1966). The prescription commences to run from the day when the voyage is terminated in the case of voyage charterparties, from the day when the contract expires or of its definitive interruption in the case of time charterparties or of bareboat charterparties (Article 4 of Decree 31 December 1966).

It must be noted that the parties may fix shorter prescription periods (Article 1 of Law 18 June 1966); however, they cannot extend such a period (Article 2220 of the Civil Code). Once the prescription period has expired, the parties may waive the prescription already matured.

With respect to contracts for carriage of goods, similar rules apply. All actions against the carrier are prescribed one year after the day when the goods have been handed over or placed at the disposal of the consignee (Articles 52 and 56 of Law 18 June 1966). Such period cannot be modified by agreement (Article 29 of Law 18 June 1966 and Article 2220 of the Civil Code).

Actions against the shipper or the consignee are equally prescribed one year after the day stipulated for delivery (Article 26 of Law 18 June 1966 and Article 55 of Decree 31 December 1966). Such a period may be shortened by agreement.

Germany

Claims against the carrier are subject to the extinction period of one year according to Article 3, paragraph 6, section 4 of the Hague-Visby Rules. Claims against the shipper for payment of freight are extinguished after four years.

Greece

Claims arising out of a contract of affreightment, i.e. for the non-performance or inadequate performance of such contract (failure to provide a seaworthy ship, failure of the ship to become an arrived ship within the agreed time or within a reasonable time, etc.), except for loss of or damage to cargo, become time-barred after a period of one year (Article 289, section 4 of the CPML) beginning from the end of the year in which the prescription period started to run (Article 291, section 1 of the

CPML). According to Article 251 of the Civil Code, the prescription period begins to run as of the time when the claim arose and was actionable.

When a co-ownership has been established, one or more persons, who need not be co-owners, may be appointed to manage the co-ownership. A manager must render accounts at any time upon a decision of the majority, and in any event annually. The right of contesting the accounts is extinguished after the expiration of one year from their approval by the majority.

Hong Kong

Pursuant to section 4(1)(a) of the Limitation Ordinance 1965, the time bar for all simple contracts is six years from the date of the cause of action.

India

The time limit is three years.

Ireland

Such claims are governed by the six-year limitation period appropriate to claims arising out of breach of contract. (Statute of Limitations 1957, s. 11).

Italy

The prescription period is one year for the charter by demise (Article 383 of the Navigation Code) and runs from the expiry of the contract or the delivery of the ship if it occurs later. It is also one year for the time charter from the expiry of the contract or the end of the last voyage if it occurs later (Article 395 of the Navigation Code). For the voyage charter the period is one year from the delivery of the goods or the date when they should have reached their destination except for inter-Mediterranean voyages or voyages between a Mediterranean port and a European port (even if outside the Mediterranean), in respect of which the prescription period is six months (Article 438 of the Navigation Code).

Japan

1. The time limit for claims by a shipowner against a charterer (except a charterer by demise), shipper, consignee or a holder of a bill of lading, is one year from the day on which the claims accrued and became due (Commercial Code, s. 765).

1. For other claims the time limit is five years from the day on which the claims accrued and became due (Commercial Code, s. 522).

Korea

1. The prescription period for charter by demise is five years (Article 64 of the Commercial Code).

1. The extinction period for other types of breach of a contract of affreightment is one year (Articles 811 and 812–6 of the Commercial Code).

Malta

The general rule in respect of claims for breach of contract is that such claims are barred by the lapse of five years. Actions for payment of freight are barred by the lapse of one year from the completion of the voyage (section 544(a) of the Commercial Code).

Mexico

The prescription period is one year from the date the claim becomes exigible (Article 159 Ley de Navegacìon).

Netherlands

1. The time-bar period is one year (Civil Code, Art. 8:1711). This period applies both in respect of claims against and by the carrier. In respect of actions founded on a time charter the period in principle commences to run from the day following the day on which the performance of the contract has ended. In respect of actions founded on a voyage charter the period in principle commences to run from the day following the day on which the voyage has ended (Civil Code, Art. 8:1717). The exceptions to this rule relating to the time of commencement, however, are numerous. In the case of an action brought by the consignor against a carrier in respect of failure to make the ship available, the period commences to run from the day following the day on which the ship should have been made available (Civil Code, Art. 8:1713).

In a number of cases mentioned in Article 8:1714, the period commences to run from the day following the day of delivery, such as in the case of an action in respect of payment of freight and in respect of delay in the time of delivery.

For actions in respect of damage sustained as a result of notice of termination or anticipated termination of contract, the period commences to run from the day following the day on which the contract has ended (Civil Code, Art. 8:1716).

For actions in respect of damage sustained by the carrier as a result of loss of or damage to the ship, the period commences to run from the day following the day on which the loss or damage occurred (Civil Code, Art. 8:1719).

2. For a carrier or consignor (including the addressee and consignee) seeking recourse against a party to the contract of carriage or contract of affreightment to recover amounts owing by him to a third party, a new time-bar period commences to run with a length of three months.[23] This rule is laid down in Article 8:1720 and will hereinafter be referred to as the "plus three months rule for the recourse action".

Norway

The general three-year time limit will apply. For contract claims of this nature, the period commences to run from maturity of the claim. If the maturity date is agreed in advance, there is no problem; otherwise the date of the default will at the same time constitute the maturity date for the compensation claim as a result of the default. If the default is accelerating a previously agreed maturity date, the three-year time limit commences to run only from the date the claimant notifies the debtor that he will invoke the default as an acceleration reason. If he fails to notify in this way, the original maturity date will constitute the commencement of the three-year time limit.

Poland

Any claim under the contract of carriage of cargo by sea is prescribed at the expiration of two years from the day when it falls due (Article 103, section 1 of the Maritime Code).

Portugal

Pursuant to Article 460 of Decree-Law No. 191/87 of 29 April 1987, any action arising out of the breach of the contract is barred after two years from the date when the claimant has become aware of his right.

23. A simple example may elucidate this. Consignor A claims compensation from carrier X for damage to cargo. X seeks recourse against Y, whom he has contracted for the carriage. To prevent the party seeking recourse (X in our example) from being able to exercise his right of recourse on account of his no longer being able to institute his recourse action in due time, namely within the time-bar period, the law allows him a new period of three months. This new period of three months commences to run on the commencement of the day following *the first of the* following days: (a) the day on which X has satisfied A's claims; (b) the day on which A has brought an action against X; (c) the day on which the time-bar period in respect of A's action against X has been interrupted; and (d) in any case the day on which the time-bar period of A's action against X has run out, no account being taken of any extension which may have been agreed between A and X.

Russia

The time limit is one year (Article 305 of the Merchant Shipping Code).

Spain

Actions for payment of freight and related expenses are subject to a six-month prescription period as per Article 951 of the Commercial Code. The time counts from the day the cargo was delivered at the contractual destination.

This short period applies to contracts of affreightment not by demise and documented either by charter parties or bills of lading (time charterers; trip charters, voyage charters, consecutive voyage charters, tonnage agreements, or carriage of cargo in a general cargo ship).

The Tribunal Supremo has clearly held that demurrage (and possible damages for detention) are "related expenses", thus, subject to the same six-month period of prescription.[24]

Contracts by demise (bareboat charter or any other demise charters) are leasing contracts. The claim for payment of hire may thus be subject to the prescription period provided by Article 1966.2 of the Civil Code, i.e. five years. The general prescription period for contractual obligations (15 years) may also be applicable to certain actions arising from lease agreements.

Sweden

The general period of time bar is 10 years. An exception to this rule might be found in a situation in which the owner/carrier is able to limit his liability in accordance with the London Convention of 19 November 1976, in which case the applicable time bar would be one year.

Switzerland

All actions arising out of a contract of hire (bareboat charter) or of affreightment (charterparty) are prescribed after one year starting from the expiry of the contract (Article 85, section 2, of the Maritime Code).

Turkey

Claims against the shipowner or the carrier are subject to a prescription period of one year from the date on which they become due (Articles 1259, paragraph 1, 1260, paragraph 1 and 1261 of the Maritime Code).

The prescription period for claims against the shipper in respect of payment of freight, etc. is one year. (Article 1262, paragraph 5 of the

24. Judgments of 17 September 1922 and of 17 January 1930.

Commercial Code). This period begins to run from the date on which the payment becomes due (Article 128 of the Code of Obligations).

United Kingdom

The time limit for actions founded on simple contract is six years from the date of breach. This applies to the following breaches of contracts of affreightment (including demise charters, time charters, voyage charters, tonnage agreements, carriage of cargo in a general ship):

—failure to make the ship available
—delays in the time of delivery
—unjustified withdrawal
—unseaworthiness
—payment of freight
—damage to the ship
—demurrage and dispatch, etc.

United States

These are maritime contracts and laches applies.[25] The period commences to run from the date of the breach of the contract.[26]

Venezuela

The time limit in respect of claims for freight both under voyage charter-parties and bills of lading is six months from the date of delivery of the goods in respect of which the freight is payable (Article 889 of the Commercial Code).

The time limit in respect of claims for demurrage is five years from the date the claim becomes exigible (Article 893 of the Commercial Code).

6. LOSS OF OR DAMAGE TO CARGO UNDER CHARTER-PARTIES AND BILLS OF LADING

Uniform Rules

Under the 1924 International Convention for the Unification of Certain Rules of Law Relating to Bills of Lading (the Hague Rules), which applies to contracts of carriage covered by bills of lading or similar documents "formant titre pour le transport des marchandises par mer", but does not apply to bills of lading issued under a charterparty unless they have been put into circulation, "in any event, the carrier is discharged from liability

25. See page 9 above.
26. Schoenbaum, see note 5 at page 10 above, 100.

unless suit is brought within one year after delivery of the goods or the date when the goods should have been delivered" (Article 3, paragraph 6, sub-paragraph 4).

Delivery of the goods occurs when they are handed over to the consignee or to his agent. For the purpose of this provision, delivery cannot be deemed to have occurred when the goods are handed over to an authority or other third party who is not acting as agent for the consignee.

The goods, the delivery of which is relevant are those covered by the contract of carriage the breach of which is alleged. Delivery must be deemed to have taken place, for the purpose of establishing when the time commences to run, at the moment when it is completed.

There is no international uniformity in respect of the legal nature of the one year period. In the United Kingdom it has been held that the one year period is a substantial remedy[27] because it extinguishes the claim and not merely the action.

Lord Wilberforce so stated[28]:

> But, and I do not think that sufficient recognition to this has been given in the Courts below, it is a time bar of a special kind, *viz*, one which extinguishes the claim (*cf.* Art. 29 of the Warsaw Convention, 1929) not one which, as most English statutes of limitation (e.g. the Limitation Act, 1939, the Maritime Conventions Act, 1911) and some international conventions (e.g. the 1910 Collision Convention, art. 7) do, bars the remedy while leaving the claim itself in existence.

In France it has been qualified as a prescription period[29] and since in French law prescription affects the action, the lapse of the period extinguishes the action, and not the right. In Italy the period is qualified by the prevailing jurisprudence[30] as a "déchéance", the legal nature of which differs from that of the prescription and, contrary to the prescription, may be waived or extended.

It is, however, clear that the only manner in which the lapse of the one-year period may be prevented is the commencement of a legal action. When a legal action may be deemed to be commenced depends on the rules in force in each country. In some countries (e.g. the United Kingdom) it is sufficient that a writ be issued, provided service is effected within a specified period of time; in others (e.g. France, Italy) service of proceedings is required in order that a legal action be deemed commenced.

The question whether the one year period may be extended has been expressly regulated by Article 1 of the 1968 Protocol to the 1924 Convention

27. *The Aries Tanker Transportation* v. *Total Transportation Limited—The Aries* (H.L.) [1977] 1 Lloyd's Rep. 334.

28. *Ibid.* at page 326.

29. Rodière, Traité Général de Droit Maritime, *Affrètements & Transports*, Tome II, Paris 1968, p. 425, No. 782; Cour d'Appel de Paris, 3 November 1982, *Europa Afrika Linie* v. *Diakhite and Others*, 1983 *Le Droit Maritime Français* 418.

30. Corte di Cassazione, 18 June 1987, No. 5357, *S.p.A. Navigazione Alga* v. *S.A.S. Rhin et Moselle*, 1988 *Il Diritto Marittimo* 1107.

pursuant to which the rule on the time bar (Article 3, paragraph 6, sub-paragraph 4) has been replaced by the following:

Subject to paragraph 6 bis the carrier and the ship shall in any event be discharged from all liability *whatsoever* in respect of the goods, unless suit is brought within one year of their delivery or of the date when they should have been delivered. *This period may, however, be extended if the parties so agree after the cause of action has arisen.*[31]

Since the cause of action arises concurrently with the loss of or damage to the goods, in practice an argument on the extension of the time limit is valid and binding if made on or after redelivery.

In the jurisdictions in which the theory of deviation applies, the time bar set out in Article 3 paragraph 6 may not operate in cases where the carrier has committed a geographical deviation. If the deviation is treated as a repudiation and, as a consequence, the original contract becomes inapplicable, as Lord Wright stated in *Tate & Lyle Ltd.* v. *Hain Steamship Company, Ltd.*,[32] the Hague Rules may not apply and the carrier is liable as a common carrier.

Paragraph 6 *bis*, reference to which is made in the new sub-paragraph 4 of paragraph 6, regulates the time bar of recourse actions, and so provides:

An action for indemnity against a third person may be brought even after the expiration of the year provided for in the preceding paragraph if brought within the time allowed by the law of the court seized of the case. However, the time allowed shall be not less than three months, commencing from the day when the person bringing such action for indemnity has settled the claim or has been served with process in the action against himself.

Pursuant to this rule, in cases where States Parties do not expressly provide a time limit for recourse actions, the three-month time limit of paragraph 6 *bis* applies. The time limit for an action for indemnity is not equal to the sum of the two time limits, *viz.* 15 months, but may be substantially longer. In fact, the one-year time limit may be interrupted by the issuance—and not the service—of a writ whilst the three months additional time limit for recourse actions commences to run from the date of settlement or of service of process. Moreover, the one-year time limit may be extended one or more times. Another question that arises in connection with sub-paragraph 6 *bis* is whether the three-month time limit operates even if the claim is settled after the expiry of the one-year time bar. It is thought that this question must be answered affirmatively, and that it will be an issue on the merits that relating to the right of indemnity of the carrier who has settled a claim which was extinguished.

Under the Hamburg Rules, which apply to contracts of carriage irrespectively of a bill of lading being issued or not, but, as the Hague Rules,

31. The words in italics have been added to the original text by the Protocol.
32. 55 Ll.L.Rep. 159, at p. 178.

do not apply to bills of lading issued under a charterparty unless they are put into circulation, "any action is time barred if judicial or arbitral proceedings have not been instituted within a period of two years" (Article 20).

The time bar is, therefore, double of that under the Hague Rules. This extension of the period does not seem to have any justification. In fact, a longer time bar creates uncertainty as to whether claims in respect of loss of or damage to goods are still outstanding and increases the difficulty of finding the facts that are relevant for the purpose of establishing whether or not the carrier is liable. In view of the fact that it is possible to request extensions, which are normally granted, and that in order to bring an action not much preparation is required, it seems to be rather unlikely that the one-year time limit may be prejudicial to the consignee. The experience gained during the long period of application of the Hague Rules constitutes the best possible evidence of this. Contrary to the Hague Rules, the time extinguishes the action and not the substantive right.

Express rules are set out in paragraphs 2 and 3 of article 20 as respects the commencement of the limitation period. Paragraph 2 so provides:

> The limitation period commences on the day on which the carrier has delivered the goods or part thereof, or in cases where no goods have been delivered, on the last day on which the goods should have been delivered.

The notion of delivery of the goods may differ from that which has been expounded in respect of the Hague Rules, for Article 4 of the Hamburg Rules, setting out the period of responsibility of the carrier, cannot be ignored. It seems in fact that redelivery must be identified with the end of the period of responsibility of the carrier. This would lead to the result that in the cases mentioned in Article 4, paragraph 2(b)(ii) and (iii) and particularly in this latter case where the carrier hands over the goods "to an authority or other party to whom, pursuant to law or regulations applicable at the port of discharge, the goods must be handed over", the limitation period may commence to run prior to the consignee actually having become aware that a loss or damage has occurred.

The reference to the delivery of part of the goods obviously covers the situation of short delivery. The provision that the period commences to run on the day on which the carrier has delivered the goods, may leave some uncertainty in a case where delivery does not take place in one day only, but continues for two or more days. The correct solution, however, must be that time commences to run from the day when delivery is completed.

Nor is any clarification brought, in respect of the case where no goods have been delivered, by the statement that time commences "on the last day" on which the goods should have been delivered. The reference to the "last day" seems to imply that if the goods had not been lost or misdelivered, there would have been a period of several days during which they should have been delivered or, in other words, a final date by which delivery should have taken place. This situation is unlikely to occur, unless a time for delivery had been expressly agreed.

Paragraph 3 then provides that the day on which the limitation period commences is not included in the period. This provision, rather strange by itself, must be considered in conjunction with that of paragraph 2, whereby the period commences "on the day" on which the carrier has delivered the goods and not "from the day" of delivery: in this latter case the time would commence to run on the day following delivery.

Paragraph 4, similarly to the new text of paragraph 6, sub-paragraph 4, of Article 3 of the Hague Rules, provides that the limitation period may be extended. The wording, however, is different in that, whilst in the Hague Rules it is stated that the parties may agree to extend the period "after the cause of action has arisen", in the Hamburg Rules it is stated that the person against whom the claim is made may grant an extension "at any time during the running of the limitation period". Whilst the reference to the running of the limitation period clearly implies that the cause of action has arisen because the period commences on delivery, the reference to the person "against whom the claim is made" seems to indicate an additional condition in order that an extension of the time limit may be obtained, namely the making of a claim. Then the question arises as to how the claim must be made: is a simple notice that a loss of or damage to the goods has occurred sufficient? Or must an express claim be made, with the indication of the amount claimed?

Paragraph 5 of Article 20 corresponds to paragraph 6 *bis* of Article 3 of the Hague Rules.

Argentina

The prescription period is one year from the date of discharge or the date when discharge should have been completed (Article 293 of the Ley de Navegacìon).

Australia

For loss of or damage to cargo carried out of Australia or between States of Australia under bills of lading the limitation period is one year from the time of discharge, or from the time when discharge should have occurred (Carriage of Goods by Sea Act 1991 (Cth), Sch, Art. 3, R. 6).

For loss of or damage to cargo carried under bills of lading into Australia from overseas, the limitation period provided for by the law of the country where the goods are shipped to would be applied.

For loss of or damage to cargo carried under charterparties, any limitation period provided for in the charterparty would be regarded as valid. In the absence of such provision, the limitation periods set out on page 71, above, in respect of contracts of affreightment apply.

Belgium

The time limit is one year from the date the goods have been, or should have been, delivered (Article 266 of the Commercial Code, Book II).

Actions for indemnity against a third person may be brought even after the expiration of the one-year period, if brought within the time allowed by the law of the court seized of the case, such time to be no less than three months, commencing from the day when the person bringing such action for indemnity has settled the claim or has been served with process in the action against him.

Brazil

The applicable prescription period is one year from the date of termination of the voyage.

Canada

See the general comment for contract claims at page 48 above except that

(a) the Hague Rules apply compulsorily to shipments from Canada under bills of lading (but not charterparties) to restrict the freedom to contracts,
(b) Canadian courts in the past have also enforced Hague and Hague-Visby limitations compulsorily applicable in other countries of shipment, and
(c) in Quebec, in situations where the provisions of the new Civil Code apply. In these cases, the prescriptive limitation has been set at one year.

On 6 May 1993 the new Carriage of Goods by Water Act (COGWA) came into force. The Act is immediately implementing the Hague Rules, as amended by the 1968 and 1979 Protocols, and provides that the Hamburg Rules will come into force on a date to be fixed by order of the Governor in Council made on recommendation of the Ministry of Transport. Section 4 of the Act provides that the Ministry of Transport shall, on or before 31 December 1999 and thereafter every five years, consider whether the Hague-Visby Rules should be replaced by the Hamburg Rules.

Chile

Claims for loss of or damage to cargo under charterparties and bills of lading are prescribed after two years from the complete, or incomplete, delivery of the goods or, in case of non delivery, from the end of the last day in which they should have been delivered (Article 1248–1249, nos. 1 and 2 of the Commercial Code).

The right to compensation for damages resulting from delay in delivery expires if no written notice is given to the carrier within 60 days from the date when the goods were delivered to the consignee (Article 1029 of the Commercial Code).

China

Paragraph 1 of Article 257 of the Maritime Code provides that the period of time within which claims with regard to carriage of goods by sea should be lodged is one year, commencing from the date on which the cargo is or should have been delivered by the carrier.

If, before or after the expiration of the one-year time limit, the person allegedly liable lodges a claim for recourse against a third person, that claim is time-barred at the expiration of 90 days, counting from the date on which the duplicate of the bill of complaint delivered by the court handling the claims against him is received by him.

Croatia

Claims for loss of or damage to cargo under charterparties and bills of lading are time-barred after a period of one year (Article 679, paragraph 1 of the Maritime Law). The time-bar period runs

(a) in the case of damages due to shortage, loss or damage to the cargo—from the date the cargo has been delivered or should have been delivered at destination;
(b) in the case of damages due to delay—from the day the cargo has been delivered (Article 679, paragraph 5, point 1 of the Maritime Law).

After a claim has arisen the parties may agree in writing to extend the time-bar period (Article 679, paragraph 3 of Maritime Law).

Finland

The time limit is one year from the date the goods have been or should have been delivered.

France

Actions in respect of loss of or damage to goods are prescribed after one year in the case of a contract of affreightment (Article 4 of Law 18 June 1966). Also, in this case a shorter period may be adopted by contract (see laws cited above, under paragraph 5). The period commences to run from the date of completion of discharge or from the date of termination of the voyage in voyage charters (Article 4 of Decree 31 December 1966); from the date of the expiry of the contract or of its definitive interruption in the case of time or bareboat charters—see laws cited above under paragraph 5, at page 73 above.

The prescription period is equally one year for the contract of carriage of goods (Article 32 of above Decree). It cannot be shortened (Article 29 of Law 18 June 1966). The period commences to run from the day when the goods have been handed over to or placed at the disposal of the consignee or when they ought to have been handed over (Articles 32 and 56 of Law 18 June 1966).

As respects contracts of carriage there exists a special regime for recourse actions (Article 32 of Law 18 June 1966). Such actions may be brought beyond the one-year prescription period provided they are brought within three months of the commencement of the action against the person principally liable or of the day when he has amicably settled the claim. Tribunals interpret this provision in a strict manner: they have held that the action is foreclosed if it is brought more than three months after the commencement of the principal action, even if the one-year prescription period has not elapsed for the claimant.

No similar regime exists as respects affreightment. The recourse actions of the person principally liable must be brought within the ordinary one-year prescription period.

Germany

German law provides for both an *Ausschlussfrist*; (section 612 Abs. 1 HGB) and a *Verjährungsfrist*[33] (section 901, number 4 HGB). As both periods of one year are met by bringing a claim before a court the effect of this period is that of an extinction period.

Greece

Claims against the carrier under a contract of carriage for loss of cargo as well as delay in performance, and frustration of the voyage, become time-barred after a period of one year (Article 289, section 4 of the CPML)

33. See page 3 above.

beginning from the end of the year in which the prescription period started to run. According to Article 251 of the Civil Code, the prescription period begins to run as of the time when the claim arose and was actionable.

Claims for partial loss of, or damage to cargo are subject to a special time limit of one year beginning from the receipt of the goods (Article 148 of the CPML). The one-year prescription period, stipulated in Article 148 of the CPML, has given rise to much controversy. In theory, it is argued that the period referred to in Article 148 of the CPML is defined therein as an extinctive time limit. However, the courts have decided that the above period is an extinctive time limit with the result that Article 261 of the Civil Code, which refers to prescription, does not apply to these claims and therefore, the one-year prescription does not begin to run again from the last act of procedure.[34] It is argued that Article 261 of the Civil Code is incompatible with the nature of extinctive time limits. In particular, in the above case it was held that whenever an extinctive time period is fixed for the exercise of a right in the sense that the omission of its exercise within the above period results in the extinction of that right, in such a case the exercise of the right within the extinctive time period entails its preservation.

Moreover, it is worth mentioning that in cases where the total or partial loss of, or the damage to, the cargo is caused by an unlawful act, whether wilful or negligent, the claim in tort is time-barred after the lapse of a period of five years from the time when the damage and the person liable to pay compensation have become known to the claimant.[35] In other words, if the claim can be founded either on contract or on tort and the claimant elects to bring an action in tort, Articles 289, section 4 and 148 of the CPML do not apply.

The Hague Rules as amended by the 1968 and 1979 Protocols have been ratified by Greece pursuant to Law 2107 of 1992 and came into force on 19 June 1993.

Hong Kong

The time bar is one year from the date of delivery.

India

In respect of claims under a bill of lading to which the Hague Rules apply the time limit is one year from the date the goods have been, or should

34. Areopagus, Judgment No. 116/89.
35. Piraeus Court of Appeal, Judgment No. 697/80.

have been delivered. Otherwise the time limit is three years from the date the claim accrued.

Ireland

The general period of limitation of six years appropriate to breach of contract claims applies.

However by the Merchant Shipping Act 1947, the Hague-Rules 1924 may apply, in which case a time bar of one year after delivery of the goods or the date when the goods should have been delivered applies.

Legislation is now in preparation to enact the Hague Visby Rules into Irish law. (Part IV Merchant Shipping (Liability of Shipowners and Others) Bill 1992).

Italy

Except when the Hague-Visby Rules apply, the prescription periods are one year or six months.

The prescription period is one year for the charter by demise (Article 383 of the Navigation Code) and runs from the expiry of the contract or the delivery of the ship if it occurs later. It is also one year for the time charter from the expiry of the contract or the end of the last voyage if it occurs later (Article 395 of the Navigation Code). For the voyage charter the period is one year from the delivery of the goods or the date when they should have reached their destination except for inter-Mediterranean voyages or voyages between a Mediterranean port and a European port (even if outside the Mediterranean), in respect of which the prescription period is six months (Article 438 of the Navigation Code).

When the Hague-Visby Rules apply the period is one year but it is debated whether its legal nature is that of prescription or of limitation of action. The prevailing view is that it is a limitation of action.[36]

Japan

For carriage in respect of which either the port of loading or the port of discharge is a foreign port, the prescription period is one year from the day on which the goods were delivered (International Carriage of Goods by Sea Act, s. 14).

For other carriages

(a) where there is no bad faith of the carrier, the prescription period is one year from the day on which the goods were delivered, or where the goods were lost, from the day on which

36. Court of Cassation 24 July 1969, no. 2798, *Ditta Carlo Tonolo* v. *Provveditorato al Porto di Venezia*, 1969 Dir. Mar., 294).

the goods should have been delivered (Commercial Code, ss. 766 and 566);

(b) where there is bad faith of the carrier, the prescription period is five years from the day on which the claims accrued and became due (Commercial Code, s. 522).

Korea

The extinction period is one year from the date of the delivery of the goods or the date when they should have been delivered. The parties, however, may agree to extend this period (Article 811 of the Commercial Code).

Malta

Under the Civil and Commercial Code actions for the delivery of goods are barred by prescription by the lapse of one year from the arrival of the vessel (section 544(e) of the Commercial Code). Although there is no judicial authority re claims for damages to cargo, we feel that the correct interpretation is that section 544(e) applies to short delivery and not to damages to goods in transit. Thus, an action for the recovery of damages to cargo is prescribed after the lapse of five years in terms of section 2156(f) of the Civil Code, and no action shall lie against the master for loss of or damage to the goods, if such goods have been received without protest and the loss or damage was visible (section 545(a) of the Commercial Code). The rules stated above are subject to the Hague Rules as a more recent special law.

Under the Carriage of Goods by Sea Act 1954[37] the carrier and the ship are discharged from all liability in respect of loss or damage unless suit is brought within one year after delivery of the goods or the date when the goods should have been delivered. Unless notice of loss or damage and the general nature of such loss or damage be given in writing to the carrier or his agent at the port of discharge before or at the time of the removal of the goods into the custody of the person entitled to delivery thereof under the contract of carriage, or, if the loss or damage be not apparent, within three days, such removal shall be *prima facie* evidence of the delivery by the carrier of the goods as described in the bill of lading. The notice in writing need not be given if the state of the goods has at the time of their receipt been the subject of joint survey or inspection (Article III, Rule 3 of the Carriage of Goods by Sea Act 1954—Chapter 140).[38]

37. This Act incorporates into Maltese domestic law the Hague Rules and applies to outward shipments.

38. If the charterparty and the bill of lading make reference to the Hague Rules, then the prescription periods under the Hague Rules are operative by incorporation in a contract.

Mexico

The prescription period, in respect of claims for loss of or damage to goods carried under a bill of lading, is six months from the date the goods have been or should have been delivered.

Netherlands

1. For actions in respect of loss of or damage to cargo under charter parties the time-bar period is one year commencing to run from the day following the day of delivery (Civil Code, Art. 8:1711 in conjunction with Art. 1714).

For a carrier or consignor (including the addressee and consignee) seeking recourse against a party to the contract of carriage or contract of affreightment to recover amounts owing by him to a third party, a new time-bar period commences to run with a length of three months, in accordance with the "plus three months rule for the recourse action" under Article 8:1720.[39]

2. As regards actions in respect of loss of or damage to cargo under bills of lading, Article 3, paragraph 6 of the Hague-Visby Rules, as incorporated in Article 8:1712 of the Civil Code, is applicable. This Article 8:1712—which provides for an extinction period of one year—also applies to carriage covered by a bill of lading not falling within the scope of the Hague-Visby Rules. Pursuant to Article 8:1712, paragraph 2, an action for indemnity against a third person may be brought even after the expiration of the year if brought within three months, commencing from the day on which the person bringing such action for indemnity has settled the claim or has been served with process in the action against himself.

Norway

Claims for damages for loss of, or damage to, or in connection with, goods (including damages for delay), and damages for incorrect or incomplete statements in a bill of lading are time-barred one year after the day the goods were delivered or should have been delivered. Claims for damages for loss suffered by cargo being delivered without presentation of a bill of lading or to the wrong person are time-barred one year after the day the goods should have been delivered, or from the day when they were delivered if this was done later.

Poland

Any claims upon the carrier in respect of the cargo resulting from the bill of lading are prescribed at the expiration of one year from the day on

39. See page 76 above.

which the cargo has been or should have been delivered. This period may, however, be extended if the parties so agree after the cause of action has arisen (Article 103, section 1 of the Maritime Code).

Portugal

If a bill of lading has been issued, the time limit is one year as provided in Article 3.6 of the Brussels Convention of 25 August 1924.

Whenever the loss of or damage to the goods has occurred before loading or after discharge, the prescription period is two years from the date when the claimant has become aware of his right, as provided by Article 27.2 of Decree-Law no. 352/86 of 21 October 1986.

Russia

The time limit is one year (Article 305 of the Merchant Shipping Act).

Spain

There is a one-year prescription period applicable to all actions for damages arising out of non-delivery, loss of or damage to goods or delay. The prescription period counts from the day of the delivery or the day in which such delivery should have taken place, according to the contract. A notice of protest for loss or damage has to be given by the receiver at the moment of delivery (apparent damages) or within 24 hours (non-apparent damages). Failing such protest the right to claim is lost (Article 952.2 of the Commercial Code).

The situation is different when Law 22 December 1949 on maritime transport documented by bills of lading applies. This is the law enacted to implement the Hague Rules in Spanish Law and has to be combined with the 1968 and the 1974 Protocols as published in the *Boletin Oficial del Estado* of 11 February 1984. This particular legislation applies only to international maritime transports documented by bills of lading when:

(a) the bill of lading is issued in a contracting State;
(b) the transport commences in a contracting State;
(c) there is a "paramount clause" incorporated in the bill of lading.

When Law 22 December 1949 applies, the situation as regards prescription is as follows:

(a) the period is one year for claims arising out of loss of or damage to the cargo;
(b) the failure to make the protest does not bar the action, but only has some effects on the *onus probandi* (see Article 22 of the Law);
(c) the Tribunal Supremo has clearly established that this period is not properly a period of prescription. It is a period of *caducidade*

(*déchéance*). This means that there is no possibility of interruption. The action is barred after one year and the judge will establish *ex officio* the *caducidade*.

Sweden

Suit must be brought within one year after the goods have been delivered, or if not delivered, one year after such time when they ought to have been delivered. (The Hague-Visby Rules as implemented).

Switzerland

All actions arising out of loss or damage to cargo under a charterparty are prescribed after one year starting from the expiry of the contract (Article 85, section 2 of the Maritime Code).

When cargo is carried under a contract of carriage by sea (*Seefrachtvertrag*), usually documented by a bill of lading, then the one-year prescription period commences with the time the goods were or should have been delivered to the receiver/consignee (Article 85, section 2 of the Maritime Code).

Turkey

In Turkish law there are two different time-bar periods, *viz.* extinction periods and prescription periods which are both one year. If the extinction period expires, the prescription period also loses its validity. The one-year prescription period commences to run from the time of discharge or from the time when discharge should have occurred.

United Kingdom

In relation to bills of lading, the Carriage of Goods by Sea Act 1971, giving effect to the Hague-Visby Rules, provides that an action for loss or damage to cargo must be brought within one year of their delivery or of the date when they should have been delivered (Hague-Visby Rules Article III, Rule 6). The parties may, however, agree to extend this period. Article III, Rule 6 does not apply to an action for indemnity against a third person (Hague-Visby Rules Article III, Rule 6 *bis*).

The 1971 Act does not apply to charterparties (Hague-Visby Rules Article V). It is open to the parties to incorporate the Act or the Hague-Visby Rules into a charterparty by inserting a Clause Paramount.

In circumstances where the Hamburg Rules apply, the limitation period is two years commencing from the day when the goods or part thereof have been delivered or the last day on which the goods should have been delivered (Hamburg Rules, Art. 20). It is open to the parties to extend the limitation period by agreement.

United States

If the Carriage of Goods by Sea Act, 46 U.S.C., ss. 1300–1315, applies then the prescription period under the statute of limitations is one year, 46 U.S.C., s 1303(6). If the Harter Act, 46 U.S.C. ss 190–196, applies laches will be followed.[40] The period commences to run when the last item of cargo is delivered, if cargo is damaged; and from the date the cargo should have been delivered, if cargo is lost.[41]

Venezuela

1. In the case of non-delivery, the action is prescribed after one year of the vessel's arrival, always provided that the ship has been lying at anchor for a 15-day time period, at least, within that same yearly period, at the port of discharge. If the vessel has not been lying at anchor for such period, actions against the carrier do not become time-barred at the expiry of one year. Once this yearly period has elapsed, the time bar does not apply until completion of the 15th day of the vessel lying at anchor at the relevant port of discharge (Commercial Code, Art. 890).

2. In the case of damage to the goods, the relevant legal action becomes extinct (*caducidade*) if the notice of such loss is not given within a 72-hour time limit running from receipt of the goods in question. Where the consignee becomes aware of the damage, prior to storage of the goods in the customs premises, either because the packages were opened in his presence, or due to his having had knowledge of the accident that occurred, the 72-hour term starts to run from the date on which the damage became known (Commercial Code, Articles 895.1, and 896). Similarly, the legal action becomes extinct if, the relevant claim having been filed and notified in time, no court proceedings are commenced within 30 days following such notification (Commercial Code, Art. 895.2).

7. CONTRACTS OF CARRIAGE OF PASSENGERS (EXCEPT DEATH OR PERSONAL INJURY AND LOSS OF OR DAMAGE TO BAGGAGE)

Argentina

Article 345 of the Ley de Navegacìon provides as follows:

Actions arising out of the contract of carriage of passengers and their luggage are prescribed at the expiration of one year from the date of the landing of the

40. See page 9 above.
41. Schoenbaum, see note 5 at page 10 above, 379.

passenger or, in the event of death, from the date when he would have landed. If the death of the passenger takes place subsequent to the landing, the prescription commences to run as of the date of the death, and the term cannot be longer than three years from the date of the accident.

Australia

Any limitation period provided for in the contract would be regarded as valid (if properly brought to the passenger's attention before the contract was made). In the absence of such provision, the limitation periods set out on page 65 above apply.

Canada

Freedom of contract will allow the parties whatever provision they choose, so long as it is not contrary to public order. In the absence of specific provision, the prescription varies from province to province, but basically it is three years under the new civil law provision in Quebec and six years in most of the common law provinces from the date the claim/cause of action arose, although in British Columbia there is a two-year prescription period.

Chile

Claims for passage money are prescribed six months after the date they became due or from the termination of the voyage (Article 1246 of the Commercial Code).

Claims for non-performance of the voyage are prescribed six months after the cancellation of the voyage, or from the occurrence of the events that prevented its performance or continuation (Article 1249, no. 3 of the Commercial Code).

Claims for damages due to delay are prescribed two years after the time when the delay occurred.

China

The Maritime Code has no special stipulations in this regard. Articles 135 and 137 of the General Principles of Civil law should apply and the time bar period as provided therein is one year, counting from the date on which infringement of a right is or should have been known.

Croatia

In respect of claims under a contract of carriage of passengers such as payment of fare, non-performance of the voyage, delays, etc. the time-bar period is two years (Article 679, paragraph 2 of the Maritime Law).

According to Article 617 of such law, the passenger must present his request to the shipowner within three days from the day the carriage ended if in territorial waters and within seven days if in foreign waters. If the passenger in these periods has given written notice to the owner, he can commence the action according to Article 679 of the Maritime Law.

Denmark

The time limit is five years from the day the claim falls due.

France

Save with respect to personal injuries or loss of, or damage to baggage, there are specific provisions only for delay. Actions for damage due to delay brought by passengers are prescribed in two years from the day when the passenger has or should have disembarked (Articles 39 and 41 of Law 18 June 1966 and Article 74 of Decree 31 December 1966).

In respect of other actions, both of the passenger and of the carrier, the general prescription seems to apply.[42] Actions of the passenger shall thus prescribe in ten years (Article 189 bis Code de Commerce as amended by Law 3 January 1977). Actions of the carrier shall prescribe in 30 years (Article 2262 of the Civil Code), except when the passenger is a merchant on a professional voyage, in which case the 10-year prescription shall apply.

Germany

For all claims the time limit is two years.

Greece

Claims arising out of a contract for the carriage of passengers for non-performance or improper performance become time-barred after a period of one year (Article 289, section 4 of the CPML) beginning from the end of the year in which the prescription period started to run (Article 291, section 1 of the CPML). According to Article 251 of the Civil Code, the prescription period begins to run as of the time when the claim arose and was actionable.

Ireland

The appropriate period of limitation is the general period of limitation of six years which applies to claims for breach of contract (Statute of Limitations 1957, s. 11).

42. See Rodière, *Affrètement et Transports*, No. 1199.

Italy

The prescription period is one year, except when the carriage commences and terminates within the Mediterranean or within Europe, in which case the prescription period is six months (Article 418 of the Navigation Code).

Japan

1. For claims of a carrier against a passenger the time limit is one year from the day on which the claims accrued and became due (Commercial Code, ss. 786, 765).
2. For claims of a passenger against a carrier the time limit is five years from the day on which the claims accrued and became due (Commercial Code, s. 522).

Korea

The prescription period is five years (Article 64 of the Commercial Code).

Malta

The general rule in section 2156(f) of the Civil Code is applicable. Actions of carriers by land or water within the limits of Malta, that is from one island to the other or from one part of an island to another part of the same island, for the payment of hire or wages are barred by the lapse of one year according to section 2147(d) of the Civil Code.

Netherlands

The time-bar period is one year commencing to run from the day following the day on which the passenger has or should have disembarked from the vessel (Civil Code, Art. 8:1750). In case of affreightment for the carriage of persons this period commences to run from the times as mentioned in Articles 8:1713, 1716 through 1719. See pages 75 and 76 above.

Norway

The general three-year time limit is applicable. See, further, at page 76 above.

Poland

The Athens Convention on Carriage of Passengers by Sea has been ratified by Poland. According to Article 176, section 1 of the Maritime Code the rules of this Convention are applicable in cases of death or personal injury to passengers or damage to their luggage (including Article 16 of this Convention governing prescription for actions).

The claims other than those governed by the Athens Convention are prescribed after a lapse of two years (Article 182 of the Maritime Code).

Portugal

The prescription period applicable is two years from the date of disembarkation or from the date disembarkation should have taken place (Article 16.2 of Decree-Law no. 349/86 of 17 October 1986).

Spain

The claim for payment of the passage money is prescribed after six months from the day on which the passenger arrives at his destination or the payment of the passage money falls due (Article 951.2 of the Commercial Code).

It may be considered by analogy that the other actions arising from the contract of carriage are subject to the same six-month prescription period. However, it may also be argued that in the absence of specific commercial rules, the prescription should follow the general rule for contractual obligations, i.e. fifteen years.

Sweden

The general period of time bar—10 years—is applicable.

Switzerland

Claims not covered by the scope of the 1974 Athens Convention are time-barred after a prescription period of 10 years.

Turkey

For all claims in respect of non-performance of the voyage or delays, the prescription is one year from the day on which the claim falls due (Articles 1259 and 1261 of the Commercial Code).

Claims against the passengers for the payment of passage monies are subject to an extinction period of one year (Article 1262, paragraph 5 of the Commercial Code). This period commences to run from the day on which the claim falls due (Article 128 of the Code of Obligation).

United Kingdom

The time limit for contractual claims is six years. The Unfair Contract Terms Act 1977 will apply to any terms which attempt to restrict time limits in such contracts (as discussed at page 55 above).

United States

These are maritime contracts and laches applies.[43] The period commences to run from the date of the breach of the contract.[44]

8. DEATH OF OR PERSONAL INJURY TO PASSENGERS AND LOSS OF OR DAMAGE TO BAGGAGE UNDER A CONTRACT OF CARRIAGE OF PASSENGERS BY SEA

Uniform Rules

Article 16 of the 1974 Athens Convention provides for a general time-bar period of two years. For the first time in a multilingual convention, the French word "prescription" corresponds in the English text to "time bar". The equivalence between these two terms is confirmed by the Hamburg Rules in Article 20, paragraph 1 of which the words "Any action . . . is time-barred" are used in the English text and the words "*Toute action . . . est prescrité*" are used in the French text.

The date from which the time bar commences to run is specified in paragraph 2 of Article 16. Such date is that of disembarkation of passengers in case of personal injury, that when the passenger should have disembarked in case of death occurring during carriage and that of the death in case of personal injury occurring during carriage and resulting in death, provided, however, in this latter case, the period does not exceed three years from the date of disembarkation.

In the case of loss of or damage to luggage, the date from which the time commences to run is the date of disembarkation or that when disembarkation should have taken place, whichever is later. The scope of application of this latter provision is not entirely clear. In fact, in the Convention a distinction is made between cabin luggage and other luggage which is not carried by the passenger in his cabin. Article 8 provides in fact for different limits of liability and Article 15 for different times when the notice of loss or damage must be given. Such time is that of disembarkation of the passenger for cabin luggage and that of re-delivery for other luggage.

Even if in this case the word "disembarkation" is not qualified, as in Article 15, paragraph 1(a)(i) and in Article 16, paragraph 3 where reference

43. See page 9 above.
44. Schoenbaum, see note 5 at page 10 above, 100–101.

ence is made to the "disembarkation of the passenger", it is thought that also in paragraph 2(c) of Article 16 the "disembarkation" to which reference is made is that of the passenger. It follows that there does not seem to be an express provision as to the moment when the time bar commences to run in respect of luggage which is not cabin luggage. On the basis of Article 15, paragraph 1 the relevant moment should be that of delivery.

As in many other international Conventions, the grounds of suspension and interruption of the limitation periods are governed by the *lex fori*. The limitation periods, however, may not, as a consequence of suspension or interruption, exceed three years from the date when disembarkation should have taken place, whichever is later. A certain degree of uniformity has, therefore, been achieved.

Argentina

Article 345 of the Ley de Navegacìon provides as follows:

Actions arising out of the contract of carriage of passengers and their luggage are prescribed at the expiration of one year from the date of the landing of the passenger or, in the event of death, from the date when he would have landed. If the death of the passenger takes place subsequent to the landing, the prescription commences to run as of the date of the death, and the term cannot be longer than three years from the date of the accident.

Australia

(a) For personal injury to passengers:

(i) For *in personam* actions:
—New South Wales, Queensland, South Australia, Tasmania and Northern Territory:
Three years.[45]
—Victoria, Western Australia:
Six years.[46]

(ii) For *in rem* actions:
—New South Wales, Queensland, Western Australia, Tasmania and Northern Territory:
No limit.[47]
—South Australia:

45. Limitation Act 1969 (NSW), s. 18A; Limitation of Actions Act 1974 (Qld), s. 11; Limitation of Actions Act 1936 (SA), s. 36(1); Limitation Act 1974 (Tas), s. 5(1) and Limitation Act 1981 (NT), s. 12(1)(b).

46. Limitation of Actions Act 1958 (Vic), s. 5(1)(a); Limitation Act 1935 (WA), s. 38(1)(c)(vi).

47. Limitation Act 1969 (NSW), s. 22(1); Limitation of Actions Act 1974 (Qld), s. 10(6)(a); Limitation Act 1974 (Tas), s. 8(1) and Limitation Act 1981 (NT), s. 20(2).

Three years.[48]

(b) For actions arising from the death of passengers:

(i) For *in personam* actions:
—New South Wales, Queensland, Tasmania and Northern Territory:
Three years.[49]
—Victoria:
Six years.[50]
—Western Australia:
One year, or six months after the deceased's representative took out representation, whichever is the later.[51]

(ii) For *in rem* actions:
—New South Wales, Queensland, Tasmania and Northern Territory:
No limit.[52]
—South Australia:
Three years.[53]
—Victoria:
Six years.[54]

(c) For actions arising from damage to, or loss of, baggage:

—Any limitation period provided for in the contract would be regarded as valid (if properly brought to the passenger's attention before the contract was made). In the absence of such provision, the limitation periods set out at page 65 above apply.

Belgium

The prescription period in the case of a passenger's injury or death is 30 years (Article 2262 of the Civil Code) or a shorter period in case of a valid agreement between the contracting parties, e.g. of a valid reference on the ticket to general conditions of the carriage of passengers providing inter alia a short time limitation.

48. Limitation of Actions Act 1936 (SA), s. 36(1).
49. Limitation Act 1969 (NSW), s. 19; Limitation of Actions Act 1974 (Qld), s. 11; Limitation Act 1974 (Tas), s. 8(1) and Compensation (Fatal Injuries) Act 1974 (NT), s. 9.
50. Wrongs Act 1958 (Vic), s. 20(1).
51. Fatal Accidents Act 1959 (WA), s. 7(1), Law Reform (Miscellaneous Provisions) Act 1941, s. 4(3)(b).
52. Limitation Act 1969 (NSW), s. 22(1); Limitation of Actions Act 1974 (Qld), s. 10(6)(a); Limitation Act 1974 (Tas), s. 8(1).
53. Wrongs Act 1936 (SA), s. 21.
54. Wrongs Act 1958 (Vic), s. 20(1).

The prescription period in respect of passengers' luggage and their motor vehicles is the same unless the luggage or motor vehicles are carried under a bill of lading; in such latter case, the time limit is one year.

Brazil

The prescription period is one year from the date of termination of the voyage.

Canada

Section 649 of the Canada Shipping Act 1936 provides a 12-month (one-year) prescription in the case of death:

> Not more than one action lies for and in respect of the same subject matter of complaint, and every action shall be commenced not later than twelve months after the death of a deceased.

Personal injury and baggage claims would be subject to the prescription discussed at page 93 above.

Chile

In cases of personal injury, claims are prescribed two years after the date of disembarkation of the passenger (Article 1249, no. 3 of the Commercial Code). In cases of death, two years from the date when the passenger should have disembarked. If the death occurred subsequent to disembarkation, but due to injuries sustained during transportation, the period starts from the date of the death, but the total period starting from the time of disembarkation cannot exceed three years (Article 1249, no. 3, of the Commercial Code).

Claims for loss or damage to baggage are prescribed two years after the date of disembarkation of the passenger (Article 1249, no. 3 of the Commercial Code).

China

The Maritime Code provides in Article 258 that the period of time within which all claims regarding carriage of passengers by sea should be lodged is two years, counting respectively as follows:

(a) Claims for personal injury: counting from the date on which the passenger disembarks or should have disembarked.
(b) Claims for death of passengers occurring during the period of carriage: counting from the date on which the passengers concerned should have disembarked. Where passengers die as a result of injuries sustained during the period of sea carriage, the

"time" should begin to count from the date of the death of the passengers concerned, provided that the whole period should not be more than three years from the time of disembarkation.

(c) Claims for loss of or damage to passenger's baggage: counting from the date on which the passenger disembarks or should have disembarked.

Croatia

The time-bar period for personal injuries or death of a passenger as well as for damage and loss of baggage is two years (Article 679, paragraph 2). The period can be extended by written agreement after the claim has arisen (Article 679, paragraph 3). The time-bar periods run as follows:

(a) in cases of personal injury—from the day the passenger disembarked.

(b) in case of death of a passenger in the course of carriage—from the date the ship arrived or should have arrived in the port in which the passenger would have disembarked.

(c) in cases of death of a passenger after the contract of carriage has terminated but as a result of injuries, sustained during the voyage—from the day of death, unless the period exceeds three years from the day the passenger has disembarked.

(d) in cases of registered baggage i.e. the baggage delivered for carriage—from the day the baggage was delivered or should have been delivered at the port where the passenger disembarked or should have disembarked.

(e) in cases of cabin baggage i.e. hand baggage—from the day the passenger disembarked or in the case of death of the passenger during the voyage, from the day the ship arrived or should have arrived at the port where the passenger intended to disembark.

Passengers' motor vehicles are considered to be baggage and thus the rule of Article 679, paragraph 2 of the Maritime Law will be applied.

Denmark

The time limit for claims for passenger injury or death is two years from the day the passenger disembarked or should have disembarked, or from the day of death, but no later than three years from the day of disembarkation (section 291, subsection 1, Rule 3 of the Danish Merchant Shipping Act).

The time limit for claims for loss of or damage to passenger's luggage is two years from the day the luggage was discharged or should have been discharged (section 291, subsection 1, Rule 4 of the Danish Merchant Shipping Act).

Finland

In respect of claims for death of or personal injury to passengers, the time limit is two years from disembarkation. In cases of death on board, time runs from when the passenger should have disembarked. In cases of death after disembarkation, time runs from the date of death, but the maximum period is three years after disembarkation.

In respect of loss of or damage to luggage and motor-vehicles, the time limit is two years from the time when they have been brought or should have been brought ashore.

France

Actions for personal injury to passengers are prescribed after two years from the day when the passenger has or should have disembarked (Articles 41 of Law 18 June 1966 and 74 of Decree 31 December 1966).

In case of death of the passenger, the two-year period commences to run from the date of the death, but may not exceed three years from the date of disembarkation (Article 74 Decree 31 December 1966, paragraph 2).

Actions for loss of or damage to baggage are prescribed after one year from the date of disembarkation of the passenger or from when he ought to have disembarked (Article 46 Law 18 June 1966 and 77 Decree 31 December 1966).

Germany

The prescription period is two years, as provided by the 1974 Athens Convention.

Greece

Claims against the carrier by sea in respect of

(a) passengers' injury or death,
(b) their luggage,
(c) their motor vehicles or
(d) goods are subject to the one-year time limit referred to at page 73 above.

In cases where the 1974 Athens Convention (ratified by Greece pursuant to Law 1922/1991) applies, claims arising out of death and personal injury of passengers and loss of, or damage to luggage are prescribed after a period of two years (Article 16 of the Convention) beginning:

(a) in case of personal injury, from the date of the passenger's disembarkation (Article 16, section 2(a));
(b) in case of death, from the date on which the passenger should have disembarked (Article 16, section 2(b));
(c) in case of personal injury during carriage which resulted in the death of a passenger after his disembarkation, from the date of his death, provided that the period does not exceed three years from the date of disembarkation (Article 16, section 2(b));
(d) in case of loss of, or damage to the passenger's luggage, from the date of disembarkation or from the date when the passenger should have disembarked whichever occurred later (Article 16, section 2(c)).

In any case, the action cannot be filed after the lapse of a period of three years from the date of the passenger's disembarkation or from the date when the passenger should have disembarked, whichever occurs later (Article 12, section 3). However, the time-bar period may be extended by written agreement between the parties or by a written statement of the carrier to this effect after the cause of action has arisen.

It has been held by the Areopagus[55] that in cases where claims arising out of loss of life or personal injury of passengers or loss of, or damage to goods can be founded either on contract or on tort because the damage to a third party was caused by an illegal act or omission, whether wilful or negligent, the action in tort is independent from the action based on contract. Consequently, if the third party elects to bring an action in tort, his claim will be time-barred after a period of five years from the time when the damage and the person liable to pay compensation became known (Article 937 of the Civil Code).

Hong Kong

The time bar in cases of death is three years from the date of knowledge of the person in whose benefit the action was brought, whichever is later (Limitation Ordinance 1965, s. 28(2)). The time bar in case of personal injury is three years from the date of the cause of action accrued or the date of the plaintiff's knowledge of the injury, whichever is later (Limitation Ordinance 1965, s. 27(1)(4)).

India

The time limit is three years from the date when the cause of action arises.

55. Judgment Nos. 660/1971 and 967/1973.

Ireland

Ireland is not a party to any international convention covering the carriage of passengers and their luggage by sea. The time limit for an action claiming damages for death caused by the wrongful act of another (otherwise than caused in a collision) is also three years (section 11(2)(b) of the Statute of Limitations 1957). Claims for loss of life or injury caused by a collision must be commenced within two years (section 46 (2) of the Civil Liability Act 1961).

The period of limitation for a claim for damage to baggage under a contract of carriage is six years (section 11(1) of the Statute of Limitations 1957).

Legislation is now in preparation (The Merchant Shipping (Liability of Shipowners and others) Bill 1992) which will give effect to the 1974 Athens Convention and will provide that any action for damages arising out of the death of or personal injury to a passenger or, for the loss of or damage to luggage, shall be time-barred after a period of two years from the date of disembarkation or, if the passenger has died during carriage, from the date when he should have disembarked or, if the passenger has died after disembarkation as a result of personal injury occurring during carriage, from the date of his death, provided that such period does not exceed three years from the date of disembarkation.

In the case of loss of or damage to luggage the limitation period shall be calculated from the date of disembarkation or from the date when such disembarkation should have taken place, whichever is the later.

Italy

The prescription period is one year, except when the carriage commences and terminates within the Mediterranean or within Europe, in which case the prescription period is six months (Article 418 of the Navigation Code).

Japan

The time limit is five years from the day on which the claims accrued (Commercial Code, s. 522).

Korea

The time limit (prescription) for actions arising from death of and personal injury to passengers is five years (Article 64 of the Commercial Code).

The time limit (extinction) for actions arising from loss of or damage to baggage is one year (Article 830(2)(3) of the Commercial Code).

Malta

The general five year limit in respect of contract claims is applicable.

Mexico

The prescription period is one year from the date when the claim is exigible (Article 1043.3 of the Commercial Code and Article 159 of the Ley de Navigacíon y Comercio Maritimo).

Netherlands

1. For actions against the carrier in respect of death and personal injury the time-bar period is three years (Civil Code, Art. 8:1751), commencing to run from the following times:

—In the case of personal injury, from the day following the day of the accident.
—In the case of death, from the day following the day of the death. However, this period will not exceed five years commencing from the day following the day of the accident.

2. For actions in respect of loss of or damage to cabin or hand baggage the time-bar period is one year commencing to run from the day following the day on which the passenger has or should have disembarked from the vessel (Civil Code Art. 8:1750).

3. The actions referred to in (a) and (b) are extinguished if the party entitled has failed to report the occurrence of the event or accident to the carrier within a period of three months. This period commences to run from the day following the day of the event or accident (Civil Code, Art. 8:1753).

This period is not applicable if:

—the party entitled has made a claim in writing against the carrier within the said period;
—the event or accident is to be imputed to the carrier;
—the event or accident has not been reported (within the said period) due to circumstances for which the party entitled is not responsible;
—the carrier has otherwise within this period become cognizant of the event or accident.

4. For a carrier, or a contracting party of the latter, or a passenger, seeking recourse against a party to the contract of carriage or contract of affreightment to recover amounts owing by him to a third party, a new

time-bar or extinction period commences to run with a length of three months, in accordance with the "plus three months rule for the recourse action".[56]

Norway

The time limit for claims for death or personal injury is two years from the day on which the passenger should have disembarked or did disembark; if the death took place after disembarkation, the time limit is two years from the day of death, but not more than three years from disembarkation.

The time limit for claims for damages for loss of or damage to luggage is two years from the day the luggage should have been brought ashore or was brought ashore. For claims for damages for delay the time limit is two years from the day the luggage was brought ashore or delivered.

Poland

1. Any claim for damages resulting from the death of, or personal injury to a passenger is barred after two years; in the event of a passenger's death, this period runs from the day on which the passenger should have disembarked, and in case of personal injury from the day on which he has disembarked (Article 176 of the Maritime Code).

In the event of the passenger's death occurring after the completion of the voyage, the limitation period begins to run from the day of the death, but may not exceed three years from the day on which the passenger disembarked (Article 176.2 of the Maritime Code).

2. Any claim for damages resulting from the loss of, or damage to baggage is barred at the expiration of six months from the day on which the baggage was, or should have been delivered (Article 176.3 of the Maritime Code).

3. If the baggage is covered by a bill of lading, the time limit is one year. If covered by a ship or ferry ticket, the claim, as any other claim under the contract of carriage, is barred at the expiration of two years from the day on which it becomes exigible (Article 99.1 of the Maritime Code).

Portugal

The prescription period applicable is two years from the date of disembarkation or from the date disembarkation should have taken place (Article 16.2 of Decree-Law no. 349/86 of 17 October 1986).

56. See page 76 above.

Russia

The civil liability of the carrier for death of or personal injury to a passenger is not determined by the provisions on the contract of carriage, but by the law of tort (Article 174 of the Merchant Shipping Code) and, therefore, claims against the carrier become time-barred after three years.

The claims arising out of a contract of carriage of luggage in foreign navigation become time-barred after one year (Article 305 of the Merchant Shipping Code).

There is no special time bar for claims arising out of carriage of a motor vehicle belonging to the passenger. Depending on the fact of the carriage of the motor vehicle as luggage (with issuance of a luggage receipt) or as goods (with issuance of a bill of lading), the respective time bar is applied.

Spain

There are no special rules for this kind of action. The rules applicable should be those mentioned at page 96 above.

However, international maritime transport of passengers is subject to the special rules contained in the 1974 Athens Convention, which is part of the Spanish law. In such cases (Article 2 of the Convention), claims for death or personal injury or for damage to or loss of luggage, are subject to a two-year prescription (see Article 15 of the Convention).

Sweden

The time limit for claims for death of or personal injury to passengers is two years from the day the passenger disembarked or should have disembarked. If the death occurred after disembarkation, the time limit is two years from the day of death, but no more than three years from disembarkation.

The time limit for claims for loss of or damage to luggage is two years from the date the luggage was taken ashore, or if the luggage has been lost, two years from the date when the luggage should have been taken ashore.

Switzerland

The two-year prescription period of the 1974 Athens Convention applies.

Turkey

Except for collision, the prescription period in respect of the claims for the death of and personal injury to passengers is one year.

If loss of life or injury to passengers is caused by collision, the prescription period is two years from the day the passenger has or should have disembarked (Article 1259, paragraph 1 and 1261, paragraph 3 of the Commercial Code).

United Kingdom

Such claims are governed by the 1974 Athens Convention which was given the force of law by the Merchant Shipping Act 1979. The time bar is two years, commencing from the following dates:

(a) in the case of personal injury—from the date of disembarkation of the passenger;
(b) in the case of death during carriage—from the date when the passenger should have disembarked;
(c) in the case of personal injury during carriage resulting in death after disembarkation—from the date of death, provided that it is within three years from the date of disembarkation;
(d) in the case of loss of or damage to luggage—from the date of disembarkation or from the date when disembarkation should have taken place, whichever is later (Athens Convention 1974, Art. 16).

The 1974 Athens Convention is excluded from the Unfair Contract Terms Act 1977.

United States

Claims for death and personal injury to passengers. Suit for death or injury of a passenger is a tort claim and must be brought within three years from the date the cause of action accrued, 46 U.S.C., 763a. However, the ticket contract may shorten the period to a time of not less than one year, 46 U.S.C., 183b.

Claims for loss of or damage to baggage. These are maritime contracts and laches applies.[57] The period commences to run from the date of the breach of the contract.[58]

Venezuela

Claims in respect of death of, or personal injury to, passengers are prescribed after 10 years from the date of the occurrence (Article 132 of the Commercial Code and Article 1977 of the Civil Code).

Claims in respect of passengers' luggage and of motor vehicles are subject to the same rules applicable to loss of or damage to goods (see page 92 above).

57. See page 9 above.
58. Schoenbaum, see note 5 above 100.

9. INSURANCE: ALL CLAIMS UNDER A CONTRACT OF INSURANCE INCLUDING CLAIMS FOR PAYMENT OF PREMIUMS AND INSURANCE INDEMNITIES, ABANDONMENT (IF A SPECIAL TIME LIMIT IS PRESCRIBED).

Argentina

Articles 468–470 of the Ley de Navegacìon Act state:

Article 468:

Actions arising out of the maritime insurance contract are prescribed with the expiration of one year. This period commences to run:

(a) In actions for collection of premiums from the date when they become due.
(b) In actions for recovery of losses: (1) in the case of a vessel from the date of the accident and in the case of goods from the date of the arrival of the vessel or, as the case may be, from the date when she should have arrived, or, if the accident took place after those dates, from the date of the accident; (2) from the expiration of the periods fixed in Articles 458, 459 and 461 as the case may be.
(c) For actions to obtain payment of contribution to general average and of salvage reward or in cases of liability for losses caused to third parties, from the date of payment.

Article 469:

The commencement of abandonment proceedings interrupts the time limit of the action for damages.

Article 470:

The action for recovery which may be instituted by the insurer against the insured becomes time-barred by the lapse of one year from the date of payment.

In proceedings for recovery which may be instituted by the insurer against third parties the period of prescription is the same as that for proceedings started by the insured in whose rights he becomes subrogated.

If, in order to collect the compensation, the insured wishes to exercise the action of abandonment, the commencement of the action interrupts the prescription of the action of damages (see Article 469 of the Ley de Navigacìon).

The action for abandonment may only be instituted within the periods prescribed in Articles 463 and 464 of the Ley de Navegacìon Act. Article 466 of the Ley de Navegacìon reads as follows:

Judicial action. The action for abandonment, except in the case of agreement between the insurer and the insured, must be exercised judicially within the periods mentioned in Articles 463 and 464, and upon starting the action, the insured must report to the insurer all the insurances contracted on the property which he abandons. Until such declaration has been presented, the insurer is not obliged to pay the relative indemnity.

Australia

1. For claims made under a contract of marine insurance any limitation period provided for in the contract would be regarded as valid. In the absence of such provision, the following limitation periods apply.

—New South Wales, Victoria, Queensland, South Australia, Western Australia and Tasmania:
Six years.[59]
—Northern Territory:
Three years.[60]

2. For claims for payment of insurance premiums or for mutual insurance calls:

(a) For *in personam* actions:

—New South Wales, Victoria, Queensland, South Australia, Western Australia and Tasmania:
Six years.[61]
—Northern Territory:
Three years.[62]

(b) For *in rem* actions:

—New South Wales, Queensland, Western Australia, Tasmania and Northern Territory:
No limit.[63]
—Victoria and South Australia:
Six years.[64]

Belgium

The prescription period is three years from the date of the occurrence causing loss or damage (Article 32 of Law, 11 June 1874).

59. Limitation Act 1969 (NSW), s. 14(1)(a); Limitation of Actions Act (Vic), s. 5(1)(a); Limitation of Actions Act 1974 (Qld), s. 10(1)(a); Limitation of Actions Act 1936 (SA), s. 35(a); Limitation Act 1935 (WA), s. 38(1)(c)(v); Limitation Act 1974 (Tas), s. 4(1)(a).

60. Limitation Act 1981 (NT), s. 12(1)(a).

61. Limitation Act 1969 (NSW), s. 14(1)(a); Limitation of Actions Act 1958 (Vic), s. 5(1)(a); Limitation of Actions Act 1974 (Qld), s. 10(1)(a); Limitation of Actions Act 1936 (SA), s. 35(a); Limitation Act 1935 (WA), s. 38(1)(c)(v) and Limitation Act 1974 (Tas), s. 8(1).

62. Limitation Act 1981 (NT), s. 12(1)(a).

63. Limitation Act 1969 (NSW), s. 22(1); Limitation of Actions Act 1974 (Qld), s. 10(6)(a); Limitation Act 1974 (Tas), s. 8(1) and Limitation Act 1981 (NT), s. 20(2).

64. Limitation of Actions Act 1958 (Vic), s. 5(1)(a) and Limitation of Actions Act 1936 (SA), s. 35(a).

Brazil

The prescription period is one year from the date when the claim becomes exigible (Article 447 of the Commercial Code).

Chile

As respects claims for payment of premiums and insurance indemnities the period is two years from the time the obligation became due, or from the occurrence of the casualty, respectively.

As respects abandonment the period is two years from the occurrence of the casualty. In cases of constructive total loss, the assured must give notice of abandonment within three months from the date when he had actual knowledge that a constructive total loss has occurred. The notice of abandonment interrupts the prescription of the action of the assured against the insurer.

China

The Maritime Code provides in Article 264 that claims for payment of the indemnity under a contract of marine insurance are time-barred at the end of two years, counting from the date on which the accident occurs.

Croatia

All claims under a contract of insurance including claims for payment of premiums and insurance indemnities are time-barred after a period of five years (Article 728, paragraph 1 of the Maritime Law).

This period begins to run:

(a) for claims for contribution in general average and for salvage awards—from the date on which the contribution or award payable by the assured has been assessed;
(b) for claims for losses caused to third parties—from the date on which the assured has received the claim from the third party;
(c) for other claims—from the first day after the end of the calendar year during which the claim has arisen.

Denmark

The time limit is two years from the end of the year in which the claimant acquired knowledge of the claim and of its falling due provided he knows where the debtor is, but no later than five years from the time the claim fell due (the Danish Insurance Act, s. 29, subs. 1).

Finland

The time limit is three years from the date when the assured becomes aware of his claim, but in no case in excess of ten years from the occurrence.

France

All actions arising out of the insurance contract are prescribed after two years (Insurance Code, Article L. 173–31).

The time from which the two year time limit commences to run varies according to the subject of the action (Insurance Code, Article R. 172–6):

(a) as respects the action for the payment of the premium the time runs from the date when the premium becomes due (Article R. 172–6, section 1);
(b) as respects the action for damage in the case of hull insurance, the time runs from the date of the occurrence (Article R. 172–6, section 2);
(c) as respects the action for damage to goods aiming at the payment of the insurance indemnity for partial loss or average, the time runs from the date of arrival of the ship or other means of transportation or, if the occurrence is later in time, from the date thereof (Article R. 172–6, section 2);
(d) as respects the action of the assured in the case of insurance of goods for total loss, the time runs from the date when the goods ought to have arrived at the point when the insured voyage was to come to an end (Article R. 172–6, section 2);
(e) as respects the action for abandonment, the time runs from the date of the occurrence giving rise to the abandonment or if it is provided that the action may not be commenced before the expiry of a specified period, from the date when such period expires (Article R. 172–6, section 3).
(f) When the object of the action of the assured is contribution to general average, salvage reward or recourse of third parties, the time runs from the date of the commencement of proceedings against the assured or the date of payment (Article R. 172–6, section 4).
(g) Lastly, as respects the action for reimbursement of any sums paid pursuant to an insurance contract, the time runs from the date of payment of the sum not due (Article R. 172–6 of the Insurance Code).

The abandonment must be made within three months from the date of the occurrence giving rise thereto (Article R. 172–4 and R. 172–6 of the Insurance Code). Beyond that time limit, only the action for damage may be brought. The assured, who has regularly notified the abandonment, has two years for the commencement of the action for the payment of the indemnity running from the occurrence entitling to the abandonment.

Germany

1. Notice in writing of all claims must be given to the insurers within 15 months, failing which the claims are extinguished (*Ausschlussfrist*).[65]

2. The time limit by which action must be brought before the court in respect of all claims against the insurer is five years, failing which claims are time barred (*Verjährungsfrist*).[66]

Greece

Claims for loss or damage under a marine policy become time-barred after a period of two years (Article 290, paragraph 2 of the CPML) beginning (Article 291, paragraph 1 of the CPML) at the end of the year within which the claim arises.

India

The time limit is three years from the date the claim accrued.

Ireland

The time limit is six years from the date on which the cause of action accrued.

Italy

The prescription period is one year. In respect of claims against the insurer for payment of the insurance indemnity time runs from the date of the occurrence or from the time when the assured proves he has learnt of the occurrence (Article 547 Navigation Code). In respect of claims of the insurer for payment of premium time runs from the date when the premium falls due.

Notice of abandonment for actual or constructive total loss must be given within two or four months from the date of the occurrence or the date when the assured proves to have gained knowledge of the occurrence

65. See page 2 above.
66. *Ibid.*

according to whether the occurrence has taken place in Europe or in the Mediterranean or outside such area.

Japan

The time limit for claims for insurance indemnities and reimbursement of premiums is two years from the day on which the accident occurred or the claims accrued (Commercial Code, s. 663).

The time limit for claims for payment of premiums is one year from the day on which the claims accrued and became due (Commercial Code, s. 663).

Korea

The time limit (prescription) for claims for payment of the insurance indemnity or for the return of premium is two years (Article 662 of the Commercial Code).

The time limit (prescription) for claims for payment of the premium is one year (Article 662 of the Commercial Code).

Notice of abandonment for constructive total loss must be given within a reasonable time (Article 713 of the Commercial Code).

Malta

Actions arising from contracts of insurance are prescribed by the lapse of five years from the day on which they could have been exercised (Commercial Code, s. 543).

No action shall lie against the insurers for damage occasioned to the goods, if such goods have been received without protest and the damage was visible (Commercial Code, s. 545(a)).

According to the Commercial Code, abandonment to the insurer must be made within the following time limits:

(a) six months from the day on which information of the occurrence is received, if it has happened on the coasts of Europe, or on those of Asia or of Africa in the Mediterranean, or, in the case of capture, from the day on which information is received that the prize was carried into any of the ports or places situated on the coasts mentioned above;

(b) 18 months from the aforesaid dates respectively, if the occurrence happened in, or the prize was conveyed to any other part of the world.

When the said time limits have expired, the assured cannot make the abandonment any longer (Commercial Code, s. 419).

In every case in which the right to abandon exists, and in case of any other peril the risk whereof is to be borne by the insurer, the assured must give notice to the insurer of any information which he may have received thereon. Such notice must be given without delay under pain of damages and interest (Commercial Code, s. 420).

Section 421 provides that if, upon the expiration of one year from the day of the vessel's departure, or from the day to which the last news of the vessel relates, in the case of ordinary voyages, or upon the expiration of two years, in the case of long voyages, the assured declares that he has received no news of the vessel, he shall be entitled to abandon, and to claim payment of the sum insured, without any necessity of proving the loss of the vessel. Upon the expiration of the aforesaid time limit of one year or of two years, the assured is allowed, for the purpose of commencing proceedings, the time limits set forth in section 419 above referred to.

The assured may, by means of the notice mentioned in section 420 mentioned above, either abandon, and claim from the insurer payment of the sum assured within the time fixed in the contract, or reserve his right to abandon within the time limits fixed by law (Commercial Code, s. 424).

The assured must, when making the abandonment, state all the insurances made, or caused to be made, or ordered by him, and the sums of money borrowed on bottomry or "at respondentia". In default of so doing, the time for payment, which is to run from the day of the abandonment, is suspended until the day on which the assured makes and notifies such statement, but the period prescribed for making the abandonment is not extended thereby (Commercial Code, s. 425).

In the case of arrest and restraint of princes and peoples, the assured must, without delay, give notice to the insurer of the information received. The abandonment of the property arrested cannot be made until after six months from the day of such notice, if the arrest is effected in the Mediterranean or other European sea; or until after one year, if the arrest is effected in a more distant place. Such periods commence to run from the day of the notice of the arrest. Where the goods arrested are of a perishable nature, the aforesaid periods are reduced to two months in the former case, and to three months in the latter case (Commercial Code, s. 433).

Where a vessel has been declared unfit for navigation, if within the time of two months the master is unable to procure another vessel for the reshipment of the goods and the carriage thereof to the place of destination, it shall be lawful for the assured to abandon the goods (Commercial Code, s. 440).

Mexico

The prescription period is two years from the date of the casualty (Article 81 of the Ley sobre Contratos de Seguros).

Netherlands

For all actions under a policy of insurance the time-bar period is five years. This period commences to run from the day on which the claim has become exigible (Civil Code, Art. 3:307), unless a shorter period is provided for in the contract.

Norway

Claims for payment of premium are time-barred pursuant to the general three-year time limit, see further at page 76 above.

Claims for compensation under the policy are time-barred three years after the expiration of the calendar year in which the insured gained knowledge of his claim, but never later than 10 years after the incident upon which the insured's claim is based. However the new Insurance Contract Act of 16 June 1989, No. 69 is in addition providing that in liability insurance the claim against the insurance company becomes time-barred at the same time as the claim for compensation against a liability insurer, the time limit for such a claim may actually be shorter or longer than what is stated above.[67]

Poland

Any claim under a contract of marine insurance is prescribed after a lapse of five years from the day on which the claim falls due (Article 269 of the Maritime Code).

Portugal

For all claims, excluding abandonment, failing special provisions the prescription period applicable is that of twenty years (Article 309 of the Civil Code). According to Article 620 of the Commercial Code, the time limit for the notice of abandonment to the insurer is three months from the day when the accident became known, if it occurred in European seas; six months, if it occurred in African seas, in Western or Southern Asiatic seas, or in Eastern American seas; one year, if the accident occurred elsewhere.

In case of capture or embargo by any country's order, these time limits commence to run only from expiry of all previous terms.

Russia

The time limit is two years (Article 305 of the Merchant Shipping Code).

67. *Cf.* what is stated about time bar of tort claims on page 33.

Spain

All actions arising from the contract of marine insurance are subject to a three year prescription period from the date of the contract or from the date of the accident in respect of which the indemnity is claimed as the case may be (Article 954 of the Commercial Code).

Sweden

The time limit is three years from the day the insured learned about his claim, but in no case later than 10 years.

Switzerland

The insurance claims are prescribed two years after the event giving rise to the claim (Article 46 of the Swiss Law of Insurance Contracts).

Turkey

All claims under a contract of insurance are extinguished after two years from the date on which the cause of action accrued (Article 1268 of the Commercial Code and Article 128 of the Code of Obligations).

United Kingdom

Claims under a contract of insurance are founded on simple contract and have a limitation period of six years. The Unfair Contract Terms Act 1977 does not extend to insurance contracts (Schedule 1).

United States

A marine insurance contract is maritime and laches applies.[68] The period commences to run from the date of the breach of the contract.[69]

Venezuela

The prescription period is five years from the date of the contract (Article 891 of the Commercial Code).

10. REINSURANCE

Argentina

There is no special prescription period for reinsurance actions, but if it is considered as a contract of insurance, a period of one year must be applied.

68. See page 9 above.
69. Schoenbaum, see note 5 at page 10 above 100.

Australia

The periods as specified on page 110 in respect of insurance.

Canada

While the general law (six years in common law provinces, three years in Quebec) applies where there is no other stipulation, these provisions may and often are varied by contract. In such case, limitation is most commonly one year, running from the date of loss.

Chile

The prescription period is two years from the time the insurer paid the indemnity to the assured.

China

The Maritime Code provides in Article 264 that claims for payment of the indemnity under a contract of marine insurance are time-barred at the end of two years, counting from the date on which the accident occurs.

Croatia

The Maritime Law and the Law of Obligations have no provisions regarding the contract of reinsurance. Claims under the contract of reinsurance are time-barred five years from the day on which the payment of the indemnity has been assessed by the assured, but no later than five years from the date on which the assured was obliged to pay the indemnity under a contract of insurance.

Denmark

The time limit is five years from the day the claim falls due.

France

There is no special rule as respects reinsurance. The prevailing view is that the provisions on insurance do not apply to reinsurance.[70] The general rule must, therefore, apply and all actions based on reinsurance contracts are prescribed in 10 years (Article 189 bis Code de Commerce, as amended by Law 3 January 1977).

Germany

The time limit is five years.

70. See Rodière and Lureau, *Assurances Maritimes*, p. 70, n. 3.

Greece

The time limit is the same as for insurance, since reinsurance is a special kind of insurance (Article 194 of the Code of Commercial Law).[71]

Ireland

Claims arising on contracts of re-insurance are governed by the six-year time bar applicable to all contract claims.

Italy

The prescription period is two years from the date when the occurrence on which the claim is based has taken place (Article 2952 of the Civil Code). Notice by the insurer of the claim made by the assured or of the proceedings commenced by him has the effect of suspending the running of the time until the claim of the assured has become enforceable or time-barred.

Japan

The time limit is the same as for insurance.

(a) The time limit for claims insurance indemnities and reimbursement of premiums is two years from the day on which the accident occurred or the claims accrued (Commercial Code, s. 663).
(b) The time limit for claims for payment of premiums is one year from the day on which the claims accrued and became due (Commercial Code, s. 663).

Korea

The same principles for insurance apply (Article 662 of the Commercial Code).

(a) The time limit (prescription) for claims for payment of the insurance indemnity or for the return of premium is two years (Article 662 of the Commercial Code).
(b) The time limit (prescription) for claims for payment of the premium is one year (Article 662 of the Commercial Code).
(c) Notice of abandonment for constructive total loss must be given within a reasonable time (Article 713 of the Commercial Code).

Malta

Section 543 Commercial Code is applicable: actions arising from contracts of reinsurance are prescribed by the lapse of five years from the day on which the same could have been exercised.

71. See page 113 above.

Netherlands

The time-bar period is five years. For all actions under a policy of insurance the time-bar period is five years. This period commences to run from the day on which the claim has become exigible (Civil Code, Art. 3:307), unless a shorter period is provided for in the contract.

Norway

The general three-year time limit applies.

Portugal

The same prescription period as for insurance applies. For all claims, excluding abandonment, failing special provisions the prescription period applicable is that of twenty years (Article 309 of the Civil Code). According to Article 620 of the Commercial Code, the time limit for the notice of abandonment to the insurer is three months from the day when the accident became known, if it occurred in European seas; six months, if it occurred in African seas, in Western or Southern Asiatic seas, or in Eastern American seas; one year, if the accident occurred elsewhere.

In case of capture or embargo by any country's order, these time limits commence to run only from expiry of all previous terms.

Spain

The maritime reinsurance follows the rules of marine insurance. All actions arising from the contract of marine insurance are subject to a three year prescription period from the date of the contract or from the date of the accident in respect of which the indemnity is claimed as the case may be (Article 954 of the Commercial Code).

Sweden

The time limit is the same as for insurance. See page 117, above.

Switzerland

Reinsurance claims are treated as general contracts and are not governed by the special provisions of the Swiss Law of Insurance Contracts as described above (Article 101 of the Swiss Law of Insurance Contracts). The reinsurance claims are, therefore, time-barred after the general prescription period of ten years as provided for by the general contract law.

Turkey

All claims under a contract of insurance are extinguished after two years from the date on which the cause of action accrued (Article 1268 of the Commercial Code and Article 128 of the Code of Obligations).

United Kingdom

Claims under a contract of insurance are founded on simple contract and have a limitation period of six years. The Unfair Contract Terms Act 1977 does not extend to insurance contracts (Schedule 1).

United States

Reinsurance for a marine insurance contract is a maritime contract and laches applies.[72] The period commences to run from the date of the breach of the contract.[73]

11. GENERAL AVERAGE

Argentina

The prescription period for actions arising out of general average is one year from the date of discharge. If an average bond is signed, the period is four years from the date of signature. The action for collection of the contribution indicated in the adjustment approved by the parties in an express form or by a judicial decision becomes time-barred after one year commencing from the approval of the adjustment or from the judicial decision (Articles 406 and 407 of the Ley de Navegacìon).

Australia

The time limit is three years (Admiralty Act 1988 (Cth), s. 37(1)(b)).

Belgium

The prescription period is one year from the date of the occurrence (Article 270 of the Code of Commerce, Book II).

Brazil

The prescription period is one year from the end of the voyage during which the loss occurred (Article 449.1 of the Code of Commerce).

72. See page 9 above.
73. *Ins. Co. of North America* v. *U.S. Fire Ins. Co.*, 1971 AMC 1891.

Canada

The time limit is six years in the common law provinces, three years under the new Civil Code provisions in Quebec, running from the declaration of the average.

Chile

General average must be declared within six months from the date of delivery of the goods or from the termination of the voyage (Article 1247, paragraph 1 of the Commercial Code).

The action for payment of contribution must be commenced within six months from the communication that the general average adjustment has been issued, except when the existence of a general average has been disputed, in which case the six-month period will commence to run for the person who has disputed the general average from the time when the lawsuit terminates (Article 1247, paragraph 2 of the Commercial Code).

China

Article 263 of the Maritime Code provides that claims for contribution to general average are time-barred at the end of one year, running from the date of the statement of general average adjustment.

Croatia

Claims for the payment of the contribution to general average are time-barred after one year from the day the ship arrived in the port of the termination of the common adventure in the course of which the general average act was made. The period is suspended from the day of the appointment of the adjuster until the day when the adjustment becomes final (Article 832 of the Maritime Law).

Denmark

The time limit is one year from the date of the average adjustment (the Danish Merchant Shipping Act, s. 291, subs. 1, rule 8).

Finland

The time limit is one year from the date of the adjustment.

France

Actions arising out of general average are prescribed in five years from the day when the voyage has come to an end (Article 40 of Law 7 July 1967).

Germany

The time limit is one year counted from the end of the year in which the contribution becomes due.

Greece

Claims for contribution to general average become time-barred after a period of one year (Article 289, paragraph 5 of the CPML) beginning (Article 291, paragraph 3 of the CPML) on the end of the year within which the claim arises.

India

The time limit is three years from the day when the cause of action arises.

Ireland

The time limit is six years from the date of the average bond or underwriters' guarantee.

Italy

Claims for contribution are prescribed one year after the completion of the voyage or, in the case of a circular voyage, of the contributing voyage (Article 481 of the Navigation Code).

Japan

For contribution to general average, the time limit is one year from the day on which the average adjustment was completed (Commercial Code, s.798).

Korea

The time limit (extinction period) is one year from the date when the average adjustment was completed. The parties, however, may extend this period by agreement (Article 842 of the Commercial Code).

Malta

The general time limit for contract claims is applicable—five years. No action shall lie against a freighter for general average contribution, if the master has delivered the goods and received the freight without making a protest (Commercial Code, s. 545 (b)).

Mexico

The prescription period is one year from the day when an action can be brought (Article 1043 (VIII) of the Commercial Code).

Netherlands

Actions for general average contribution become time-barred after the lapse of a period of one year from the day following the day on which notice of the average statement has been given to all the parties or on which the same have been informed that the average statement has been lodged with the court (Civil Code, Art. 8:1832).

Actions for general average adjustment and apportionment and for appointment of an average adjuster for this purpose, become time-barred after the lapse of a period of one year. This period commences to run from the day following the day on which all the cargo has been delivered.

Norway

The time limit is one year from the date of the average adjustment. The time limit for a claim for compensation for damage, loss or expense in general average is one year from the day the ship reached port after the average act, or, if the ship is lost, from the day of the average act.

Poland

Any claim arising out of general average is prescribed after a lapse of two years from the day of termination of the voyage (Article 229 of the Maritime Code).

Portugal

Pursuant to Article 1068 of the Code of Civil Procedure, the action for contribution to general average is prescribed after one year from discharge or, in case of total jettison of the goods, from the arrival of the ship at the port of destination.

Russia

There is no special time bar concerning claims arising out of general average. The average adjusters attached to the Chamber of Commerce and Industry are competent for the apportionment of general average. The persons interested may apply to the average adjuster with statements for the apportionment of general average within the general time-bar period, i.e. one year when all persons interested in the apportionment of general average are Russian entities and three years in all other cases.

The general average statement may be disputed in court by any person at interest within six months in the case of the statement of general average in foreign navigation (Article 249 of the Merchant Shipping Code). If the general average statement is not disputed within such period, or if it is disputed, but affirmed by the court, it may be enforceable in the same manner as a notarial deed (Article 250 of the Merchant Shipping Code).

Spain

Actions for general average contribution are subject to a six month prescription period. Article 951 of the Commercial Code provides that time commences from the date when the cargo was delivered. However, in practice, it is accepted that time counts from the moment the general average statement (in which the debt is clearly indicated) is completed and made known to the debtors.

Sweden

The time limit is one year from the date the Swedish Official Average Statement becomes legally binding.

Switzerland

In accordance with Article 124 of the Maritime Code, claims for contributions to general average are time-barred after a prescription period of two years from the day on which the goods arrived at the port of destination or on which they should have arrived there.

Turkey

The prescription period is one year from the date of the court decision that affirms the average adjustment (Articles 1259 and 1261 of the Commercial Code).

United Kingdom

Claims in general average have a limitation period of six years under the common law. Time begins to run against cargo owners from the date of the general average act i.e. when each general average sacrifice or expense was made or incurred.[74]

74. *Castle Insurance Co. Ltd.* v. *Hong Kong Islands Shipping Co. Ltd.* (*The Potoi Chau*) [1983] 3 All ER 706.

If, however, parties subsequently enter into an agreement under Lloyd's form of average bond, time starts to run from the date of the publication of the average adjuster's statement.[75]

United States

Generally, the statutory time within which a claim for general average may be made is governed by the laws of the port of destination. The time limit governing suits arising out of written contracts is applicable, unless it is U.S. government cargo in which case it must be brought under the Suits in Admiralty Act, 46 U.S.C. ss. 741–752, and the time limit is two years. The period commences to run from the time the ship reached its destination and the cargo was delivered, unless the voyage is abandoned in which case the date of abandonment governs.[76]

12. SALVAGE

Uniform Rules

Article 10 of the 1910 Brussels Convention for the Unification of Certain Rules of Law Relating to Assistance and Salvage at Sea (1910 Salvage Convention) provides in its first paragraph that the action for payment of the remuneration is prescribed after two years from the day when the salvage operations are terminated. In the unofficial English translation, the words "is prescribed" (*se prescrit*) are translated with the words "is barred".

This article then provides, similarly to Article 7 of the 1910 Collision Convention, that the grounds upon which the prescription may be suspended or interrupted are determined by the law of the court where the case is tried. Also in this case, as in Article 7 of the Collision Convention, the word "prescription" is translated with "period of limitation".

The last sentence of Article 10 permits Contracting States, as does that of Article 7 of the Collision Convention and that of Article 9 of the 1926 Maritime Liens and Mortgages Convention, to provide that the prescription period may be extended in cases where it has not been possible to arrest the vessel salved in the territorial waters of the State in which the plaintiff has his domicile or principal place of business. As has been pointed out when commenting on Article 7 of the Collision Convention (see page 15, above), this is a situation of suspension of the prescription period and, therefore, it is governed by the *lex fori*.

75. *Ibid.*
76. Buglass, *Marine Insurance and General Average in the United States*, 302–304 (1991).

Argentina

The period is two years starting from the date when the operations are completed (Article 385 of the Ley de Navigacìon).

Australia

For ships on international and interstate voyages: two years (Navigation Act 1912 (Cth), s. 396(1)).

For ships on intrastate voyages:

—New South Wales:
Two years.[77]
—Tasmania and Northern Territory:
Two years.[78]
—Victoria, Queensland, South Australia and Western Australia:
Three years.[79]

(NB: In each jurisdiction, the period commences from the time when the salvage services were rendered.)

Belgium

The prescription period is two years from the day when salvage operations are completed (Article 270, Code of Commerce, Book II).

Canada

Section 471 of the Canada Shipping Act 1936 provides a two-year prescription period commencing at the time the salvage services have been completed.

Chile

Actions for payment of salvage remuneration are prescribed two years after the date when the services were completed (Articles 1248 and 1249, no. 5 of the Commercial Code).

Actions for recovery by the owner of the vessel of the part of the salvage remuneration paid for the owners of the cargo are also prescribed two years after the date of the judgment or award whereby the owner has been

77. Limitation Act 1969 (NSW), s. 22(3).
78. Limitation Act 1974 (Tas), s. 8(3); Limitation Act 1981 (NT), s. 20(4).
79. Admiralty Act 1988 (Cth), s. 37(1)(b).

found liable to pay the remuneration or from the date of voluntary payment (Articles 1248 and 1249, no. 6 of the Commercial Code).

China

Article 262 of the Maritime Code provides that claims regarding salvage at sea are time-barred at the end of two years, running from the date on which salvage operations are completed.

Croatia

Claims for salvage remuneration are time-barred after two years from the day the salvage operations are terminated (Article 782, paragraph 1 of the Maritime Law). The crew, having the right to a part of the remuneration, can take legal action against the owner of a salved ship after a period of one year commencing from the date on which the salvage operation terminated (Article 782, paragraph 2 of the Maritime Law). The period can be extended by written agreement between the parties after the claim has arisen (Article 782, paragraph 3 of the Maritime Law).

Denmark

The time limit is two years from the day the salvage operations are completed (the Danish Merchant Shipping Act, s. 291, subs. 1, rule 1).

Finland

The time limit is two years from the day when the salvage operations are completed.

France

Actions for payment of the salvage reward are prescribed two years after the day when the salvage operations terminate (Article 18 of Law 7 July 1967). However, the prescription does not run if the salved vessel may not be arrested in French waters (Article 18, paragraph 2 of Law 7 July 1967).

Germany

The prescription period is two years, as provided by the 1910 Salvage Convention.

Greece

Claims for salvage become time-barred after a period of two years (Article 290, paragraph 3 of the CPML) beginning (Article 291, paragraph 1 of the same Code) upon the end of the year within which the claim arises.

According to the prevailing view,[80] claims of the master and crew of the salving vessel against the owner of such vessel for that part of the remuneration, which is due to them and which has been collected by the owner, do not come within the provisions of Article 290, section 3 of the CPML but are subject to the general rules of prescription of the Greek Civil Code (20 years from the time the claim arose and was actionable, Article 249 of the Civil Code).

Hong Kong

The time bar is two years from the date of the cause of action as under the 1992 Salvage Convention.

India

The time limit is three years from the date when the claim for salvage remuneration accrues.

Ireland

An action for salvage remuneration is not specifically time-barred by any statutory provision. Section 5 of the Civil Liability Act 1961 repealed section 8 of the Maritime Conventions Act 1911. Accordingly, no time limit applies to actions *in rem* in respect of salvage services, except in the limited cases mentioned in section 46 of that Act, i.e. where salvage expenses are recoverable as damages, caused by the sole or concurrent fault of a vessel. In addition, section 11(8)(b) of the Statute of Limitations 1957 specifically provides that the provisions of that Act do not apply to any cause of action within the Admiralty jurisdiction of the High Court which is enforceable *in rem*.

Legislation is now in preparation (Merchant Shipping (Wreck and Salvage) Bill 1992) which will provide that any action relating to payment under the law of salvage shall be time-barred after the expiry of two years from the day the salvage operations terminate.

Italy

The period of prescription is two years both when the 1910 Salvage Convention applies and when the Navigation Code Art. 500, applies. The

80. Areopagus, Judgment No. 231/57.47.

period commences to run as from the date when the salvage operations are completed.

Japan

The time limit for claims for salvage remuneration is one year from the day on which the salvage operations came to an end (Commercial Code, s. 814), but two years in cases where the 1910 Salvage Convention applies.

Korea

The time limit (extinction) is two years from the date when the salvage operations are completed. The parties, however, may extend this period by agreement (Article 860 of the Commercial Code).

Malta

The applicable period of prescription is that of five years (Civil Code, s. 2156(f)), unless the claim is based on a public deed, in which case the action would be barred after the lapse of 30 years.

Mexico

The prescription period is two years from the day when the salvage operations are completed.

Netherlands

For actions in respect of salvage remuneration, as provided for by Article 10 of the Salvage Convention (1910), the time-bar period is two years. The same time-bar period also applies, pursuant to Article 8:1820 Civil Code to:

—salvage services not falling within the scope of the 1910 Salvage Convention,
—all other actions in respect of the rendering of assistance, hence also in respect of actions against the party rendering assistance,

and commences to run from the day following the day on which the salvage operations are terminated.

This period is extended when the vessel to which such assistance has been rendered cannot be arrested within the state where the creditor resides or has its corporate domicile (Civil Code, Art. 8:1823). This provision is identical to Article 8:1792 relating to collision.[81]

Norway

The time limit is two years from the day the salvage operations are completed.

Poland

Any claim for salvage remuneration is prescribed after a lapse of two years from the day of termination of the salvage services (Article 250 of the Maritime Code).

Portugal

Portugal is a party to the 1910 Salvage Convention which was approved by law, 7 May 1913 and confirmed by law, No. 187 of 12 August 1913. Pursuant to its Article 10, the action for payment of salvage remuneration must be brought within two years from the day when the assistance or salvage operations were ended; the causes of suspension and interruption of the prescription are determined in accordance with the law of the court where the case is tried.

Russia

Russia is a party to the 1910 Salvage Convention and, therefore, the claims for salvage remuneration falling under this Convention (Article 12) become time-barred after a period of two years.

In all other cases, claims for salvage remuneration become time-barred after a period of three years. Such cases are rare, but nevertheless they are possible (e.g. a claim for salvage remuneration between the owners of vessels which fly the flag of states not parties to the 1910 Salvage Convention).

Spain

A special law (law 60/1962 of 24 December 1962) applies. This law implements the 1910 Salvage Convention. Therefore, the prescription period is two years from the moment the salvage operations are completed. However, Spain has availed itself of the provision contained in Article 10, section 3 of the 1910 Salvage Convention. Thus this period is suspended for the time the salved vessel cannot be arrested (Article 11 of Law 50/62 employs the terms "interruption of prescription", but, in fact, the effect

81. See page 19 above.

of the provision considering also that it derives from that of Article 10 of the Convention, is rather that of suspension).

Sweden

The time limit is two years from the day when the operations of assistance of salvage terminate (1910 Brussels Convention).

Switzerland

Until the coming into force of the revised provisions of the Maritime Code, salvage claims are time-barred after a two year prescription period in accordance with the 1910 Salvage Convention. Until the entering into force of the Maritime Code (presumably Summer 1993), the 1989 Salvage Convention and thereby its Article 23 (prescription period of two years) will apply.

Turkey

The prescription period is two years as provided by the 1910 Salvage Convention (Article 1259, paragraph 2 of the Commercial Code). The period commences to run from the date when the salvage operations are completed (Article 1261, paragraph 5 of the Commercial Code).

United Kingdom

The Maritime Conventions Act 1911 provides that an action in respect of salvage services must be brought within two years. Time begins to run from the date when the salvage services were rendered (Maritime Conventions Act 1911, s. 8).

United States

The time bar is two years and it begins to run on the date when the assistance or salvage was rendered. However, if the court in which suit is brought determines that during the time-bar period there were no reasonable opportunities to arrest the assisted or salved vessel within the jurisdiction of the Court or within the territorial waters of the country in which the libellant resides or has his principal place of business, then the Court may extend the time-bar period. 46 U.S.C., s. 730.

Venezuela

The prescription period is 10 years from the day when action may be brought (Article 132 of the Commercial Code).

III

TIME-BAR PERIODS FOR SECURITIES

1. MORTGAGES AND HYPOTHÈQUES

Argentina

As there is no special time limit in the Ley de Navegacìon, the general prescription period of the Civil Code must be applied, i.e. 20 years (Article 3197 of the Civil Code).

Australia

1. If the mortgage is executed by deed:

—New South Wales, Tasmania, Northern Territory and Australian Capital Territory:
Twelve years.[1]
—Queensland:
No limit.[2]
—South Australia and Victoria:
Fifteen years.[3]
—Western Australia:
Twenty years.[4]

2. If the mortgage is executed by simple contract:

—New South Wales, Victoria, Queensland, South Australia, Western Australia, Tasmania and Australian Capital Territory:
Six years.[5]

1. Limitation Act 1969 (NSW), s. 16; Limitation Act 1974 (Tas), s. 23(1); Limitation Act 1981 (NT), s. 14(1) and Limitation Act 1985 (ACT), s. 24(1).
2. Limitation of Actions Act 1974 (Qld), s. 26(6).
3. Limitation of Actions Act 1936 (SA), s. 34 and Limitation of Actions Act 1958 (Vic), s. 20(1).
4. Limitation Act 1935 (WA), s. 38(1)(e)(i).
5. Limitation Act 1969 (NSW), s. 14(1)(a); Limitation of Actions Act 1958 (Vic), s. 5(1)(a); Limitation of Actions Act 1974 (Qld), s. 10(1)(a); Limitation of Actions Act 1936 (SA), s. 35(a); Limitation Act 1935 (WA), s. 38(1)(c)(v); Limitation Act 1974 (Tas), s. 4(1)(a) and Limitation Act 1985 (ACT), s. 11.

—Northern Territory:
Three years.[6]

Canada

Mortgages are not subject to any extinction period.

Chile

As a general rule hypothèques are extinguished together with the obligation secured thereby. The judicial sale of the vessel causes the extinction of the hypothèques provided:

(a) notice of the auction is given to all holders of hypothèques, and
(b) the holders of hypothèques do not declare within 15 days that they exercise the option to keep their security in existence after the forced sale.

If they fail to make any such declaration, they are deemed to have chosen to be satisfied out of the proceeds of sale. The option is not granted if the credit secured by the hypothèque has expired (Article 879 of the Commercial Code).

The hypothèques of subsequent date are satisfied out of the balance resulting from the auction and in the portion not covered they are extinguished.

A vessel measuring less than 50 G.R.T. cannot be the subject of a hypothèque, but may be given as security, which must be noted in the margin of the entry of the vessel in the register of ships and its extinction is subject to the same rules as the hypothèque.

China

The Maritime Code has no special stipulations in this regard. Articles 135 and 137 of the General Principles of Civil Law should apply and the time bar period as provided therein is two years, counting from the date on which the breach is or should have been known. However, the mortgage as a type of security may be difficult to separate from the creditor's right secured thereby.

Croatia

Claims secured by mortgages, i.e. contractual rights of pledge (Article 201 of the Maritime Law) as well as claims secured by liens are governed by

6. Limitation Act 1981 (NT), s. 12(1)(a).

the appropriate time-bar period in accordance with the Maritime Law or the Law of Obligations, whichever is applicable.

The creditor is entitled, after the lapse of the extinction period, to enforce his claim (without interest) against the ships on which a hypothèque has been registered in the public register (Article 368 of the Law of Obligations).

Denmark

Registered mortgages, in real estate are not subject to extinction (see Land Registration Act, s. 42). Chattel mortgages and registered naval mortgages are presumably not subject to limitation or will at least usually not be subject to limitation before 20 years after registration.

France

Hypothèques are prescribed after 10 years from the date of their registration in the special register of hypothèques. However, if the period of the credit exceeds 10 years, registration can be renewed before the date of expiry.

Interest is not protected by registration in excess of two years beyond the year of registration, except special endorsement, effective from the date thereof.

Germany

Registered mortgages are not subject to any extinction period.

Greece

The extinction of a claim which is secured by a mortgage (simple or preferred) causes the extinction of the mortgage. There is no special provision in the CPML for the extinction period relating to the security itself. Consequently, by virtue of Article 204 of the CPML the relevant provisions of the Civil Code apply by analogy, with the result that the maritime mortgage is extinguished if the claim secured thereby becomes time-barred (Article 1317 of the Civil Code) or is otherwise extinguished (i.e. by waiver, set off, etc.). Further, maritime mortgages are extinguished by the lapse of the period for which they were granted (Article 1318, no. 4 of the Civil Code). Finally, in the case of a mortgage existing on a ship when she acquires Greek nationality, the mortgage is acquired by registration in a public register and is registered in the Greek mortgage register within 60 days following the registration of the ship as a Greek ship (Article 203 of the CPML).

Ireland

The Statutory Limitation periods applying to actions brought to recover any principal sum of money secured by a mortgage or charge do not apply to any mortgage or charge on a ship (Statute of Limitations 1957, s. 36 (1)(a)). It seems that in relation to ships the old rule that no period of limitation applied to a mortgage of personalty still applies.

A mortgagee does not lose his right to enforce his security against the ship by lapse of time (Statute of Limitations 1957, s. 39 and s. 4.)

Italy

The rights arising out of the hypothèque (*viz.* the right of enforcement of the security and of satisfaction with priority out of the proceeds of sale) are prescribed with the lapse of two years from the date of expiry of the debt secured thereby (Article 577 of the Navigation Code). Hypothèques on land property are extinguished if the registration is not renewed within twenty years (Articles 2878, no. 2 and 2847 of the Civil Code). It is however doubtful whether this rule applies to ships hypothèques.

Japan

Hypothèques are not extinguished by prescription in favour of the obligor and the person granting the hypothèque unless simultaneously with the claim secured thereby (Civil Code, s. 396); provided, however, that they are extinguished in favour of persons other than the obligor and the person granting the hypothèque by the lapse of 20 years from the day on which the hypothèques were constituted and the claims secured thereby beçame due (Civil Code, ss. 396 and 167 (2)).

Korea

Mortgages must necessarily be registered and they are not subject to a time-bar/extinction period.

Malta

1. *Mortgages*: The mortgage will continue to attach until it is actually discharged.

2. *Hypothèques*: Any hypothèque to which a ship may be subject under the provisions of the Civil Code shall not continue to attach to it when the vessel is transferred to third parties (Merchant Shipping Act, section 37D (2)).

A hypothèque is not effectual unless registered in the Public Registry and ranks from the date of its registration (section 2033(1) of the Civil

Code). The registration of a hypothèque in the Public Registry shall cease to have effect after 30 years from the date thereof unless such registration is renewed before the expiration of the said time (section 2053(1)). A renewal, if made after the expiration of the prescribed time shall have the effect of an original hypothèque which shall rank only from the date of the renewal (section 2054 of the Civil Code).

Hypothèques are extinguished, *inter alia*, by prescription. Prescription takes place in favour of the debtor, in respect of property of which he is in possession, by the lapse of the time established for the prescription of the debt to which the hypothèque refers (section 2085 of the Civil Code). As to property in the possession of a third party, prescription takes place in favour of such third party by the lapse of ten years from the day on which he acquired such property, even though the creditor may not have known that such property had passed into the hands of a third party (section 2086 of the Civil Code). The registration made on request of the creditor does not interrupt the running of the prescription in favour of the debtor or of the third party in possession (section 2087 of the Civil Code).

Mexico

Hypothèques are subject to a three-year prescription period (Article 126 of the Ley de Navegacìon y Comercio Maritimo).

Norway

For registered mortgages and hypothèques, the priority and protection created by the registration will elapse after 20 years from the first registration unless the registration is renewed before this time limit expires. However, in no case will the effect of the registration expire until five years after the time when the debt according to the content of the document should have been repaid in full. In other words: if the loan secured by a mortgage is running for 25 years, the effect of the registration will only expire five years thereafter, i.e. after 30 years from the first registration.

Poland

The maritime hypothèque as such is not extinguished as a consequence of the lapse of time.

Prescription of claims secured by a maritime hypothèque has no influence on the existence and validity of the hypothèque.

Portugal

Article 730 of the Civil Code provides that the hypothèque is prescribed after 20 years from its registration and after five years from the expiry of the obligation. The prescription operates only in favour of a third party purchasing the property.

Spain

The action arising out of the ship hypothèque is prescribed after 10 years from the moment in which it can be exercised, in the manner provided in the Ley de hypoteca naval (Law of Naval Hypothecation) 21 August 1893, Art. 49).

Sweden

The position according to Swedish law is that securities are not subject to the same time bars as the claims they secure.

In other words, the time bar relevant to the security is not an accessory to the time bar which relates to the claim itself. No time limit is applicable to mortgages and hypothèques under the condition that the security has become effective against third parties.

Switzerland

Hypothèques registered in the Swiss Register of Ships are not affected by any prescription period (Article 45 of the Swiss Law on Register of Ships).

Turkey

Hypothèques are not subject to any time bar period if the security is registered.

United Kingdom

The Limitation Act 1980, provides that an action to recover money secured by a mortgage must be brought within 12 years from the date on which the right to receive the money accrued (Limitation Act 1980, s. 20(1)). The limitation period in respect of foreclosure actions is 12 years from the date when the right accrued.

Hypothecation confers on the lender a maritime lien against the cargo.

Actions to enforce a lien against a vessel in collision cases in respect of loss or damage to another vessel, her cargo or property on board, personal injury or death, or in respect of salvage services, must be brought within two years from the date when the loss, damage or injury was caused or when the salvage services were rendered (Maritime Conventions Act 1991, s. 8).

The Court has jurisdiction to extend the limitation period if it is satisfied that during that period there has not been any reasonable opportunity to arrest the vessel.

Apart from the above exception, maritime liens are not subject to any limitation period for enforcement. However, such rights may be lost through lack of reasonable diligence in enforcing them.

United States

Ship mortgages which fall within the parameters of 46 U.S.C., ss 31321–31330 are maritime contracts which can give rise to maritime liens. Laches applies to causes of action arising from such mortgages. However, due to the ownership interests implicit in a mortgage, courts apply a very broad concept of laches,[7] and claims brought 10 years after the maturity of a mortgage have been held timely.[8] State statutes of limitations govern mortgages not covered by 46 U.S.C., ss 31321–31330.

2. MARITIME LIENS

Uniform Rules

There are now three international Conventions on maritime liens and mortgages: the International Convention for the Unification of Certain Rules Relating to Maritime Liens and Mortgages made in Brussels, 10 April 1926 (1926 Convention); the International Convention for the Unification of Certain Rules Relating to Maritime Liens and Mortgages made in Brussels, 27 May 1967 (1967 Convention) and the very recent International Convention on Maritime Liens and Mortgages, 1993, adopted on 6 May 1993 (1993 Convention).

The 1926 and the 1967 Conventions are both in force. The 1993 Convention is obviously not yet in force. However, since it is intended to replace the two former Conventions, it is worthwhile to also consider its provisions.

All three Conventions have provisions on the extinction of maritime liens.

1. The 1926 Convention

Pursuant to Article 9 of the 1926 Convention, the general extinction period is one year. The extinction period is six months only for liens for supplies. Different rules are set out in the second paragraph in respect of the time when the period commences to run.

7. See page 9 above.
8. G. Gilmore & C. Black, *The Law of Admiralty*, 711–712 (1975).

These, however, are not exclusive rules on the extinction of maritime liens. Article 9, in fact, contains a general reference to national laws. The application of national laws is only restricted in one situation, and that is the case where the extinction occurs as a consequence of the voluntary sale of the vessel. The Convention in fact makes the extinction conditional to the fact that the sale be accompanied by formalities of publicity, including a notice to the registrar.

The extinction periods may be interrupted in the manner provided by national law. The penultimate paragraph of Article 9 states that the grounds upon which the periods of extinction may be interrupted are determined by the law of the court where the case is tried. The provision differs from those in Article 7 of the Collision Convention and in Article 10 of the Salvage Convention because it does not make reference, in addition to interruption, to suspension of the extinction periods.

The last paragraph of Article 9 then provides that Contracting States are permitted to extend the extinction periods in cases where it has not been possible to arrest the vessel in the territorial waters of the State in which the claimant has his domicile or principal place of business. However, whilst in the 1910 Collision and Salvage Conventions such right is unlimited, in the 1926 Convention it is limited to a maximum period of three years.

The remark made in respect of the corresponding provision of the 1910 Collision Convention, that such a provision was not strictly necessary since it covered a specific case of suspension of the period, does not apply in the present case, for, as previously noted, reference to national law is made only in respect of interruption of the periods, and not in respect of suspension.

2. The 1967 Convention

The 1967 Convention has a much simpler rule. Its Article 8 paragraph 1 provides that the maritime liens shall be extinguished after a period of one year from the time when the claims secured thereby arose, unless, prior to the expiry of such period, the vessel has been arrested, such arrest leading to a forced sale.

All references to national laws have, therefore, been eliminated and the extinction of maritime liens for causes other than the extinction of the claims secured thereby is exclusively governed by the Convention. Nor can the *lex fori* apply in respect of suspension or interruption of the extinction period. This is clearly stated in paragraph 2 of this Article.

The only way of preventing the lapse of time is the arrest of the ship, provided it leads to the forced sale of the vessel. If the vessel is released, the one-year extinction period continues to run as if the vessel had never been arrested. The reason for this strict rule is that, maritime liens being secret charges, it is in the interest of third parties that they remain effective for as short a period as possible and that the period of their life be known to all.

Should an arrest after which the vessel is released because for example the claimant has obtained security, prevent the extinction of the maritime lien for the enforcement of which it had been made, third parties would not, in all likelihood, be aware that the arrest was made. The fact that in such case the arrest does not interrupt the running of the extinction period does not cause any injustice to the arrestor, for he has obtained alternative security. It would be even worse if ordinary proceedings on the merits of the claim secured by a maritime lien could prevent the running of the extinction period, for this would extend the period for a very long time without the knowledge of third parties.

If a vessel is arrested by one claimant, such arrest is effective with respect to all maritime liens that existed on the vessel at the time of arrest. It is, therefore, unnecessary for the other claimants whose claims are secured by maritime liens to re-arrest the vessel in order to prevent the extinction of their liens, provided, of course, that the arrest leads to the forced sale of the vessel.

The danger the other claimants are running is that the arrestor, if offered satisfactory security, may release the vessel. If the extinction period for other maritime liens has not yet expired the holders of such other liens may arrest the vessel. But if the vessel is released when such extinction period has expired, such other claimants would have lost their security.

Article 7 paragraph 2 of the 1967 Convention provides an exception to the general rule set out in paragraph 1. It states that the time shall not run during the period the lienor is "legally prevented" from arresting the vessel. In the draft submitted to the 1965 New York Conference of the CMI, it was provided that the time does not run when the claimant is legally prevented to arrest the vessel "owing to it having been requisitioned or to the owner being bankrupt or being in compulsory liquidation". These words were deleted because it was felt that they would unduly restrict the cases in which the claimant may be legally prevented from arresting the vessel. This wording was changed by the CMI Conference at Lisbon to "not permitted by law" in order to cover situations such as that where a vessel already under arrest may not be arrested again by another claimant.

3. *The 1993 Convention*

Article 9 of the 1993 Convention reproduces Article 8 of the 1967 Convention except that a special rule is set out in respect of the commencement of the one-year extinction period in respect of claims for wages and other sums due to the master, officers and other members of the vessel's complement, including costs of repatriation and social contributions payable on their behalf. For such claims the extinction period commences to run from the date of the claimant's discharge from the vessel.

Special rules are then set out in Article 6 in respect of national maritime liens. Whilst in fact the 1967 Convention provides in Article 6 paragraph 1 only that Contracting States may grant liens to secure claims other than those referred to in Article 4 without specifying the nature of such liens, the 1993 Convention makes clear in its Article 6 that States Parties may grant other maritime liens ranking after those set out in the Convention, but provides a six-month extinction period, which replaces the one-year period set out in Article 9.

The scope of the *droit de suite*, which is one of the most relevant characteristics of maritime liens, is substantially restricted in respect of national maritime liens. Whilst Article 8 provides that maritime liens follow the vessel, notwithstanding any change of ownership, or of registration or of flag, Article 6 provides that in case of sale to a *bona fide* purchaser of the vessel, national maritime liens are extinguished at the end of a period of 60 days unless the six-month general period expires earlier. The reference to a *bona fide* purchaser means that if it is proved that the purchaser is not *bona fide*, the 60-day extinction period does not operate and, therefore, the six-month period from the time when the claim has arisen applies.

The 60-day period commences to run on the date on which the vessel is registered after the sale.

In order to establish whether registration has been properly effected, reference must be made to the law of the State of registration.

Argentina

Argentina ratified the Brussels Convention of 1926. The extinction period does not run when there is a legal obstacle preventing the privileged creditor from arresting the ship (Article 484 (a) of the Ley de Navegacìon).

Australia

In New South Wales, Tasmania and the Northern Territory, claims on maritime liens for damage done by a ship and for salvage services are barred after two years. In these cases, both the claim and the lien are time-barred.[9]

In other jurisdictions, and for other claims on maritime liens in the above jurisdictions, claims on maritime liens are barred after three years: Admiralty Act 1988 (Cth), s. 37(1)(b). The claims secured by the maritime liens do not become time-barred simultaneously with the lien; the

9. Limitation Act 1969 (NSW), s. 22(2),(3); Limitation Act 1974 (Tas), s. 8(2),(3) and Limitation Act 1981 (NT), s. 20(3),(4).

claimant may bring an *in personam* action on the claim at any time until the expiration of the limitation period for that type of action.

Canada

From the point of view of prescription, the lien expires upon the expiry of the cause of action.

Chile

Irrespective of the extinction of the claims secured thereby, maritime liens expire:

(a) After one year from the date the claim secured thereby has accrued.
(b) By the judicial sale of the vessel concurrently with the entry of the sale in the relevant register of ships, or after 30 days from the date of the auction, whichever occurs first.
(c) In case of voluntary sale of the vessel, maritime liens expire 90 days after the date of the entry of the transfer in the ships register (Article 855 of the Commercial Code).

The right of retention terminates with the delivery of the vessel to the person who ordered the work or with the provision of security in the amount stated by the Court for the claim in respect of which the right of retention was exercised (Articles 856 and 857 of the Commercial Code).

China

The Maritime Code provides in Article 29 that with the exception of the provisions of Article 26 thereof, maritime liens on a ship shall terminate if they have not been exercised within one year running from the date on which they have arisen.

The one-year period may not be suspended or interrupted.

Article 26 of the Maritime Code provides that maritime liens are not extinguished by reason of the voluntary sale of the ship, except where they have not been exercised within 60 days from the day when a court gives notice of the transfer upon application by the transferee.

Croatia

The extinction period for maritime liens is one year and in cases of maritime liens as referred to in Article 216, paragraph 1.5 is six months. The extinction of a lien does not affect the claim secured by the lien.

Denmark

A lien expires after a period of one year from the time when the lien arose (the Danish Merchant Shipping Act, s. 248, subs. 1).

Finland

Maritime liens are extinguished if they are not enforced within specified periods.

France

Most of the maritime liens on the ship are extinguished after one year. The time limit commences to run either from the date of the enforceability of the claim, or from the date when operations have terminated in case of salvage, from the date when damage was caused for collision claims and other indemnities for property damage or personal injury, and from the date of delivery of the cargo or that when delivery should have taken place for loss of or damage to cargo or baggage (Article 39 of Law 3 January 1967 and Article 10 of Decree 27 October 1967).

Maritime liens for repairs and supplies to a ship are extinguished six months after the date when the claim has arisen (Article 39 of law 3 January 1967 and Article 10 of Decree 27 October 1967).

All maritime liens are extinguished in the case of confiscation of the ship for police or safety violations, of judicial sale and, in case of voluntary sale two months after the registration of the deed of sale (Article 40 of Law 3 January 1967).

The lien on the freight is extinguished by the payment of the freight (the freight still in the hands of the master or the agent of the owner being still subject to the lien); the lien on the accessories of the ship (lifeboats, anchors, etc.) is extinguished following the transfer of the accessory to a third party in good faith (Article 41 of Law 3 January 1967).

Germany

A maritime lien is extinguished one year after the claim secured thereby has arisen if the ship is not seized. This is an *Ausschlussfrist*.[10]

Greece

If a claim becomes time-barred, the maritime lien does not survive in any case. If the lien ceases to exist, the claim is not affected therefrom and remains valid.

10. See page 2.

Maritime liens arise in accordance with Article 205 of the CPML in respect of the claims specifically mentioned therein. They are terminated upon the ship's sale by public auction. In the event of contractual sale of the ship, the lien is preserved pursuant to Article 207 of the CPML, if within three months from the entry of the sale in the Ship's Registry, an action is brought against the new owner.

India

Maritime liens are extinguished if they are not enforced within three years from the day when they accrued.

Ireland

Section 8 of the Maritime Conventions Act 1911 has been repealed by section 5 of the Civil Liability Act 1961. The only statutory provisions applying to claims to enforce liens are in respect of claims to recover seamen's wages (section 11(8)(a) of the Statute of Limitations 1957) and claims for damage arising out of a collision (section 46 of the Civil Liability Act 1961). Such damage claims include any salvage or other expenses consequent upon the collision (section 46(4) of the Civil Liability Act 1961).

Section 11(8)(a) of the Statute of Limitations 1957 provides that an action to recover seamen's wages shall not be brought after the expiration of six years from the date on which the cause of action accrued.

Apart from this instance, the Statute of Limitations 1957 does not apply to any cause of action within the Admiralty jurisdiction of the High Court which is enforceable *in rem* (section 11(8)(b) of the Statute of Limitations 1957).

Section 46 of the Civil Liability Act 1961 which deals with liability for loss or damage arising out of a collision provides that no action shall be maintainable to enforce a claim for damages, or lien in respect of such damages, unless proceedings are commenced within two years from the date when the damage was caused. A court having jurisdiction to deal with an action under this section may extend the period within which the proceedings may be commenced to such extent, and subject to such conditions, as it thinks fit. The court is obliged to extend the period if it is satisfied that there has not been a reasonable opportunity of arresting the defendant vessel within the jurisdiction of the court within the two-year period provided for.

Maritime liens other than those arising as a result of the sole or concurrent fault of a vessel, or for seamen's wages are not limited to any time for enforcement, but travel with the ship into whosoever's possession she may come, but may be lost through lack of reasonable diligence in enforcing them. The loss of a lien through lack of reasonable diligence in its enforcement is unlikely to affect the limitation period appropriate to the substantive claim.

Italy

Italy is a party to the 1926 Brussels Convention on Maritime Liens and Mortgages, and the provisions of such Convention have force of law in Italy. Pursuant to Article 9 of the Convention maritime liens are extinguished after a period of one year except for the maritime lien for supplies which is extinguished after a period of six months. The maritime lien for salvage runs from the day when the services terminated; for collision damage and personal injury from the day when the damage was caused; for loss of or damage to cargo from the day of delivery; for repairs or supplies from the day when the claim has arisen; in all other cases the period runs from the day when the claim may be enforced. Italy has availed itself of the provision in the last paragraph of Article 9 of the 1926 Convention and Article 558 of the Navigation Code in fact provides that the period of extinction is suspended until the vessel has been arrested in the Italian territorial waters; provided, however, the period does not exceed three years.

Japan

Maritime liens against a ship are extinguished when one year has elapsed from the day on which such a claim arose (Commercial Code, s. 847(1)); provided, however, that the following maritime liens mentioned in the Commercial Code, s. 842(viii) are extinguished upon the departure of the ship (the Commercial Code, s. 847(2)):

(a) claims which have arisen from the sale or construction and the equipment of the ship, in cases the ship has not yet made any voyage after her sale or construction; and
(b) claims in respect of the equipment and food and fuel of the ship for her last voyage.

Korea

Maritime liens are extinguished one year after the date when they have arisen (Article 870 of the Commercial Code).

Malta

Maritime privileges arise by operation of the law and are enumerated in section 50 of the Merchant Shipping Act 1973, as amended by Act XXXVII of 1988. It is only the maritime privileges under section 50 of the

Merchant Shipping Act 1973 that will continue to attach to vessels, notwithstanding the sale of the ship, if the rules mentioned below have been satisfied (section 37D(2) of the Merchant Shipping Act). Privileges or hypothèques arising under the Civil Code do not attach after the sale. After a voluntary sale, maritime privileges will only continue to attach for a period of one year after the registration of that sale in the Register. If the sale is a judicial sale, maritime privileges are extinguished and the privileges only apply to the proceeds of the judicial sale. (Section 37D(3) of the Merchant Shipping Act).

Prescription takes place in favour of the debtor by the lapse of the time established for the prescription if the debt to which the privilege refers (section 2085 of the Civil Code).

Mexico

Maritime liens are extinguished when the ship starts a new voyage.

Netherlands

The privileges in respect of sea-going vessels are extinguished by the lapse of a period of one year, unless the creditor has enforced his claim at law (Civil Code, Art. 8:219). This period commences to run from the day following the day on which the claim has become exigible. In respect of a claim for salvage remuneration, however, the said period commences to run from the day following the day on which the assistance has ended.

Norway

Claims secured by maritime liens do not become time-barred simultaneously with the lien. Maritime liens against a ship are time-barred one year after the day the secured claim arose.

Poland

Poland is a party to the 1926 Brussels Convention on Maritime Liens and Mortgages. Therefore maritime liens are extinguished after one year, except the liens securing claims for supplies, which are extinguished after six months (Article 68 of the Maritime Code).

Portugal

Portugal is a party to 1926 Maritime Liens and Mortgages Convention and, therefore, the time limits set out in Article 9 of the Convention apply.

Liens on ships other than those of the Convention (Commercial Code, Art. 579) are extinguished concurrently with the extinction of the claim secured thereby, by the judicial sale of the ship, after the proceeds are deposited and by voluntary sale of the ship, notice of which has been given to the creditor, if three months have elapsed and the creditor has not enforced his lien or has not contested the price of sale.

Russia

Maritime liens are extinguished after one year from the day when the claim secured thereby has arisen (Article 235 of the Merchant Shipping Code), except maritime liens securing claims arising out of contracts entered into or acts done by the master for the preservation of the vessel or the continuation of the voyage, which are extinguished after six months (Article 280.5 of the Merchant Shipping Code).

Spain

Maritime liens are extinguished with the claim secured thereby, i.e. prescription of the claim means prescription of the maritime lien (accessoriety principle). However, the Commercial Code provides for special and independent prescription (better "*caducidade*") for maritime liens. The creditor cannot exercise his right *in rem* against the vessel after three months from the moment in which the vessel has come back to her home port (Article 582 of the Commercial Code).

In practice, this may mean a long life period for maritime liens, since the vessel often never comes back to her home port. However, Spain is a State party to the 1926 Maritime Liens and Mortgages Convention. Therefore, in all cases where the Convention applies, the maritime liens are extinguished after a period of one year, except for the maritime lien for supplies, which is subject to the shorter period of six months (see Article 9 of the Convention, where the moment from which the period starts running for each type of maritime lien is well specified).

Further, Spain has not availed itself of the provision in the last paragraph of Article 9 of the Convention. Therefore, a suspension of the time by reason of the impossibility to arrest the vessel does not seem possible.

Sweden

Maritime liens are extinguished after one year. Maritime liens provide an exception to the general rule (Brussels Conventions of 1926 and 1967).

Switzerland

Liens are extinguished, like those according to Article 9 of the 1926 Convention, at the expiration of a period of one year. But the extinction of the lien does not involve the barring of the claim itself which depends on its own particular time-bar rules.

Turkey

According to Article 1259, paragraph 1 of the Commercial Code, maritime liens are extinguished after a period of one year except for the maritime liens for collision and salvage which are extinguished after a period of two years (Article 1259, paragraph 2 of the Commercial Code). All these periods commence to run from the date on which the lien arises.

United Kingdom

Actions to enforce a lien against a vessel in collision cases in respect of loss or damage to another vessel, her cargo or property on board, personal injury or death, or in respect of salvage services, must be brought within two years from the date when the loss, damage or injury was caused or when the salvage services were rendered (Maritime Conventions Act 1991, s. 8).

The Court has jurisdiction to extend the limitation period if it is satisfied that during that period there has not been any reasonable opportunity to arrest the vessel.

Apart from the above exception, maritime liens are not subject to any limitation period for enforcement. However, such rights may be lost through lack of reasonable diligence in enforcing them.[11]

United States

The doctrine of laches[12] applies to time-bar periods for maritime liens. The time from which the period commences to run depends upon the underlying claim behind the lien. Thus, the period for a lien based on a maritime contract commences to run at the date of breach, while the period for a lien based on a maritime tort commences to run from the date the cause of action accrued.

Venezuela

There is no special extinction period for maritime liens except for the case of voluntary sale of a vessel, when all maritime liens are extinguished after 60 days from the date the vessel sailed, indicated by the buyer, save that the holders of such liens notify their opposition (Articles 617 and 618 of the Commercial Code).

11. *The Jacob* (1802) 4 Ch. Rob. 245.
12. See page 9 above.

3. POSSESSORY AND OTHER LIENS

Argentina

The civil law liens which may be enforced on the ship (lien of the fisc, of the shore-based employees, of the owner, of the registrar) are extinguished in accordance with the general rules, *viz.* together with the claim secured (save in case of transfer of the title to the ship to a third party in good faith).

The lien of the carrier on the goods carried is extinguished after the lapse of 15 days from the delivery of the goods, or following the transfer of the goods to a third party in good faith.(Article 23 of law, 18 June 1966).

Australia

There are no provisions limiting the time within which a possessory lien may be exercised.

Canada

Unlimited.

Chile

Liens on cargo are extinguished if they are not enforced within 30 days from the date the discharge was completed or by the transfer of the cargo to third parties subsequent to the discharge, even before the expiration of the said 30-day period.

However, in case of claim for freight and its accessories, including loading, discharging and storage expenses, the goods that during the period of 30 days were transferred, will continue to be subject to the lien during the eight days following delivery to the purchaser (Article 864 of the Commercial Code).

China

The rules on the extinction of maritime liens apply. See page 143, above.

Croatia

The creditor is entitled after the lapse of the extinction period to enforce his claim (without interest) against the goods in his detention.

Denmark

Possessory liens are presumably not subject to limitation.

Germany

There are no provisions limiting the time within which possessory liens may be exercised.

Ireland

The right to retain possession of the security is not affected by any time bar.

Italy

There are no provisions limiting the time within which possessory liens on ships may be exercised. Instead, with regards to possessory liens on cargo, Article 564 of the Navigation Code provides that such liens are extinguished if the claimant does not notify its opposition to the master or does not bring an action within 15 days from discharge and, in any event, before the goods that have been discharged are legally transferred to a third party.

Japan

Possessory liens are not extinguished by lapse of time.

Korea

There are no provisions limiting the time within which possessory liens may be exercised.

Malta

Any ship repairer, shipbuilder or other creditor into whose care and authority a ship has been placed shall have a possessory lien over the ship which is extinguished by the voluntary release of the ship but not if the vessel is released pursuant to a court order or following a judicial sale of the vessel. In the latter case, the creditor shall enjoy the priority specified in section 54A of the Merchant Shipping Act 1973 over the proceeds of sale of the ship (section 54 of the Merchant Shipping Act). This is a maritime privilege and the rules on maritime privileges apply for its extinction.

Maritime privileges arise by operation of the law and are enumerated in section 50 of the Merchant Shipping Act 1973, as amended by Act XXXVII of 1988. It is only the maritime privileges under section 50 of the Merchant Shipping Act 1973 that will continue to attach attach to vessels, notwithstanding the sale of the ship, if the rules mentioned below have been satisfied (section 37D(2) of the Merchant Shipping Act). Privileges or hypothèques arising under the Civil Code do not attach after the sale. After a voluntary sale, maritime privileges will only continue to attach for a period of one year after the registration of that sale in the Register. If the sale is a judicial sale, maritime privileges are extinguished and the privileges only apply to the proceeds of the judicial sale. (Section 37D(3) of the Merchant Shipping Act).

Prescription takes place in favour of the debtor by the lapse of the time established for the prescription of the debt to which the privilege refers (section 2085 of the Civil Code).

Moreover, the creditor shall be obliged to release the ship if he is paid the sum claimed, or adequate security is deposited in the Commercial Court under the provisions of the Code of Organization and Civil Procedure but, in such a case, the creditor shall enjoy the same priority over such sum.

The special lien or privilege which, under section 2009(c) of the Civil Code, is competent to the person letting the vessel or the master for the payment of the freight, extends also to average contributions and other charges (section 308 of the Commercial Code). Such lien or privilege, however, both in regard to the amount of freight, and to the average and other charges, ceases on the expiration of 15 days from the day of delivery of the goods, notwithstanding that such goods may have not yet passed into the hands of third parties. According to section 337 of the Commercial Code, the master has, for the payment of the passage money and the provisions, a right of retention over the effects brought on board by a passenger, in addition to the same special privilege as is competent to the creditors mentioned in paragraph (b) of section 2009 of the Civil Code.

The Malta Maritime Authority has a lien or privilege for the amount of all rates leviable under the Malta Maritime Authority Act 1991 (s. 40) in respect of any goods, on such goods and shall be entitled to seize and detain the same until such rates are paid in full. There is no provision on the extinction of such a lien.

Netherlands

The privileges in respect of things on board sea-going vessels, are in principle extinguished simultaneously with the delivery of the things in question to the party entitled (Civil Code, Art. 8:227).

Norway

Liens on cargo are extinguished when the goods are delivered. For executory liens, the effect of the registration lasts for only five years. For arrest and other similar injunctions, the corresponding time limit is two years. If the registration is renewed, a corresponding new time limit for the effect of the registration will apply.

Portugal

Liens on cargo (Commercial Code, Art. 581) are extinguished if the creditors do not enforce them before discharge or within 10 days thereafter, provided, during that period, the goods do not become the property of a third party.

Liens on freight are extinguished (Article 583 of the Commercial Code) when the freight is paid.

Spain

There is a general prescription period (better to say here "*caducidade*") of one year for special actions (injunctions) for recovering or retaining possession of any property (Article 1968.1 of the Commercial Code). The injunction for retaining possession could well be used by a ship repairer entitled to a possessory lien as provided in Article 1600 of the Civil Code. On the other hand, the recovering injunction could be employed by a shipowner seeking recovery of the possession of his ship.

Sweden

No time limit is applicable to the security, under the condition that the security has become effective against third parties.

Switzerland

Statutory liens secured by an entry into the Swiss Register of Ships are not affected by any prescription period (Articles 51, section 3 and Article 45 of the Swiss Law on Register of Ships).

Turkey

There are no provisions limiting the time within which possessory liens on ships may be exercised.

United Kingdom

Apart from the exceptions set out at page 149 above, liens are not subject to any limitation period for enforcement.

4. OTHER CHARGES

Canada

Assuming these to be such items as statutory liens, including liens for pilotage, harbour dues and seaway dues. From the point of view of prescription, the lien expires upon the expiry of the cause of action.

China

Chinese laws have no provisions regarding "other charges".

Denmark

Pledges are not subject to limitation.

Germany

There are no provisions limiting the time within which charges, such as the pledge, may last.

Italy

The only other charge in respect of movable property other than ships is the pledge. There is no provision on the extinction of a pledge. Article 2794 of the Civil Code provides that the person who has pledged his property cannot demand its restitution unless the debt is fully paid and all expenses relating to the custody of the pledged property are reimbursed.

Japan

Not extinguished by lapse of time.

Korea

Pledges are not subject to limitation.

Malta

The debt due to the pledgee over the movable, which he holds as a pledge, is a privileged debt. There is no provision on the extinction of a pledge. Section 1979 of the Civil Code proves that the debtor cannot claim the restitution of the thing pledged until he has wholly paid the principal, interest and expenses of the debt for which the pledge is liable.

Netherlands

For securities other than those mentioned above no special time-bar or extinction period applies. In general, the security is extinguished by the claim for the performance of which the security was provided becoming time-barred.

Norway

It may be stated that, as a general rule, the time bar of the claim is not affecting the security. However, there are certain exceptions from this principle:

(a) A non-registered pledge will be extinct at the same time as the claim that is secured by the claim. A pledge in this context means a security established by agreement between the parties. Thus, possessory, executory or other liens will not be affected by the time bar of the claim the liens are securing.
(b) In case a mortgage or other security is securing a time-barred claim, the only remedy available to the claimant is, of course to seek satisfaction against the security.

Spain

Perhaps the rule contained in Article 1962 of the Civil Code may be mentioned here. Actions *in rem* with respect to movables have a prescription period of six years as of the date when the possession was lost. This may be applicable to ships in possession of persons other than their owners.

Switzerland

Pledges are not subject to limitation. The claim secured by the pledge is not affected by this rule and will be time-barred pursuant to the applicable rule of prescription/extinction as the case may be. The expiration of the statute of limitations does, though, not prevent the obligee from exercising his right of foreclosure.

Turkey

Other charges (pledges) are not subject to limitation.

United Kingdom

An action to enforce a statutory charge is a claim for equitable relief.[13] The limitation period is 12 years, running from the date when the right to receive the money accrued.

13. *Poole Corporation* v. *Moody* [1945] KB 350.

IV

SUSPENSION OR INTERRUPTION OF THE TIME-BAR PERIODS

The period of time after the lapse of which the action is barred or the right is extinguished may be suspended or interrupted. As a general rule, in case of suspension the original time limit continues to run after the period of suspension, whilst in case of interruption a new period commences to run anew from the date of the interruption.

1. STATUTORY PROVISIONS IN RESPECT OF THE SUSPENSION OF TIME-BAR PERIODS

Argentina

As regards suspension of the prescription period, Article 3986 of the Civil Code provides:

> Prescription is interrupted by an action against the person in possession, even if commenced before a judge without jurisdiction, or, if annulled due to a formal defect or because the plaintiff did not have the legal capacity to be a party in the judicial proceedings.
> The prescription period may be suspended only once by claiming payment to the debtor through any authentic means. Such suspension will only have effect during the term of one year or during the shortest term corresponding to the prescription of the action (Article 3986).

There has been a long discussion about the application of this provision of the Civil Code to commercial claims. There is now a decision of the Supreme Court holding that Article 3986 of the Civil Code is applicable to commercial claims and as a consequence also to maritime claims.

Australia

In Victoria, Queensland, Western Australia and Tasmania: the time-bar period is suspended if the claimant is under a disability when the cause of action arises, and begins to run when the disability ceases.[1] In New South

1. Limitation of Actions Act 1958 (Vic), s. 23(1); Limitation of Actions Act 1974 (Qld), s. 29(1); Limitation Act 1935 (WA), s. 16 and Limitation Act 1974 (Tas), s. 26(1)).

Wales, South Australia and the Northern Territory: the time-bar period is suspended whenever the claimant comes under a disability.[2] A person is under a disability for these purposes:

(a) If he or she is a minor (under 18 years of age) or if she is of unsound mind (New South Wales, Victoria, Queensland, South Australia, Western Australia, Tasmania, Northern Territories)[3];
(b) If he or she is in prison (New South Wales, Queensland, Northern Territory)[4];
(c) If he or she is substantially impeded in the management of his or her affairs for a continuous period of 28 days by reason of disease or physical disability (New South Wales, Northern Territory).[5]

In New South Wales, Victoria and Tasmania, the limitation period is suspended if it is not reasonably practicable to commence an action by reason of any war or warlike operations involving the Commonwealth of Australia.[6]

Canada

The only statutory provisions in respect of the suspension of time bar/ extinction are provisions, such as those in the Quebec Civil Code, relating to impossibility to act.

Chile

The general statutory provisions regulating the suspension and the interruption of the prescription do not apply to maritime law, except the interruption mentioned below.

China

There are general rules on suspension of time-bar periods in Article 139 of the General Principles of Civil Law. Article 139 provides that time limits

2. Limitation Act 1969 (NSW), s. 52; Limitation of Actions Act 1936 (SA), s. 45 and Limitation Act 1981 (NT), s. 36.
3. Limitation Act 1969 (NSW), s. 11(3); Limitation of Actions Act 1958 (Vic), s. 3(2); Limitation of Actions Act 1974 (Qld), s. 5(2); Limitation of Actions Act 1936 (SA), s. 45(2); Limitation Act 1935 (WA), s. 40; Limitation Act 1974 (Tas) s. 2(2) and Limitation Act 1981 (NT), s. 4(1).
4. Limitation Act 1969 (NSW), s. 11(3)(b)(ii); Limitation of Actions Act 1974 (Qld), s. 5(2) and Limitation Act 1981 (NT), s. 4(1).
5. Limitation Act 1969 (NSW), s. 11(3); Limitation Act 1981 (NT), s. 4(1).
6. Limitation Act 1969 (NSW), s. 11(3)(b): if substantially impeded for a continuous period of 28 days; Limitation of Actions Act 1958 (Vic), s. 23(2) and Limitation Act 1974 (Tas), s. 28.

are suspended during the last six months of the limitation period if the plaintiff cannot exercise his right of claim because of *force majeure* or other obstacles. The time limit commences to run again on the day when the grounds for the suspension cease.

However, Article 141 of the General Principles states that when there exist special rules governing limitation, such rules apply. A special provision in respect of suspension of the limitation periods may be found in Article 267 of the Maritime Code which provides that the time bar period shall be suspended when an action is brought in the court or the case is submitted to arbitration by the claimant or when the person against whom the claim is brought agrees to fulfil his obligations. It provides further that the time limit is not suspended if the claimant withdraws his claim or his submission to arbitration or the action brought by him in the court is dismissed.

Where the claimant applies for the arrest of a vessel the time-bar period is suspended from the date on which the claim is made.

The time-bar period shall count anew from the date of the suspension.

Croatia

The statutory provisions in respect of the suspension of time-bar periods, if not regulated by the Maritime Law, are governed by the Law of Obligations 1978 (Articles 381–393). The extinction periods cannot be suspended or interrupted.

Denmark

There are no such provisions in Danish law.

France

In French law there are general causes of suspension of prescription, applicable to maritime prescriptions.

The first cause is the minor age of the claimant (Article 2252 of the Civil Code); Article 2253, never applied in Maritime Law, extends the suspension to the relationship between husband and wife. Such cause of suspension has been applied to the carriage by air. It would certainly apply also to carriage of passengers by sea as well as to carriage of goods.

In general the jurisprudence accepts the suspension of the prescription when the claimant cannot commence an action (*contra non valentem agere non currit praescriptio*). This rule has been applied in respect of the carriage

7. See page 2 above.

of goods by sea, when the behaviour of the carrier is such as to indicate to the consignee that there is no reason for him to sue him.

Germany

There are statutory provisions in respect of suspension and interruption that only relate to the *Verjährungsfrist*.[7] It is a decision from case to case whether this can be applied to an extinction period accordingly.

Greece

The Greek Civil Code (Chapter X) provides both for suspension (Articles 255–259) and for interruption (Articles 260–267) of time-bar periods. A prescription or extinction period is suspended:

(a) for the time during which the beneficiary has been prevented by reason of a *moratorium* or on account of some other case of *force majeure* from pursuing his claim within the last six months of the time-bar period;
(b) for the period of time included in the last six months of the prescription period during which the beneficiary of the prescription was fraudulently dissuaded by the debtor from pursuing the claim.

The above rules apply by analogy also to extinction periods to the extent that they are compatible with their nature and purpose.

Ireland

Chapter 1, Part III of the Statute of Limitations 1957 provides for the extension of limitation periods in the case of disability (i.e. in the event that the claimant is a person under eighteen years or is of unsound mind), acknowledgement, part payment, fraud and mistake. In such cases there is a fresh accrual of the cause of action. In the event of fraud or mistake the period of limitation does not begin to run until the claimant has discovered the fraud or mistake or could with reasonable diligence have done so.

A court may extend the time-bar period in claims arising out of a collision (Civil Liability Act 1961, s. 46(3)).

The extension period contained in the Hague Rules, Art. 3(6) may be extended by the consent of the carrier (section 13 and 2nd schedule of the Merchant Shipping Act 1947).

Israel

Under the Limitation Act the commencement of the limitation period is postponed, if the cause of action is fraud; it will start when the claimant becomes aware of the fraud. The commencement of the limitation period is also postponed as long as the creditor does not know the facts constituting the cause of action for reasons independent of him and his ignorance could not have been avoided by taking reasonable care.

If the claimant is, at the time of the accrual of the cause of action, still a minor, the commencement of the limitation period will be postponed, until he has reached the age of 18 years.

The limitation period is suspended:

(a) as long as the claimant is mentally incapable, and no guardian has been appointed for him—when a guardian has been appointed, the suspension will cease only after the guardian has become aware of the facts constituting the cause of action;
(b) as long as the claimant is the guardian of the debtor, or vice versa;
(c) as long as the parties are married to each other (if the marriage has been pronounced void *ab initio*, the parties are nevertheless deemed to have been married till the pronouncement);
(d) as long as one of the parties is in a foreign country in a position which prevents him from conducting legal proceedings, or when the relation prevailing between the country and Israel prevents him from conducting legal proceedings.

In all those cases the limitation period will not run out for at least one year after the cause of suspension has ceased; if the cause of suspension is mental incapacity of the claimant, the limitation period will not run out for at least two years after the cause of suspension has ceased.

It has been held that the provisions of the Act relating to the postponement and the suspension of the time-bar period do not apply to the time bars under the Hague Rules and the Warsaw Convention, as they are absolute.

Italy

In the Civil Code there are specific provisions on the suspension of the prescription. These provisions do not apply, unless otherwise expressly stated, to a different type of extinction period known as "Decadenza" (*Déchéance*) (Article 2964 of the Civil Code).

Prescription periods are suspended due to the relationship between the parties in the following cases (Article 2941 of the Civil Code):

(a) between spouses;
(b) between those who exercise paternal authority or powers connected therewith and the persons subject to paternal authority;
(c) between the guardian and the minor or interdict subject to guardianship until the final accounting has been submitted and approved;

(d) between the curator and the emancipated minor or other disabled person;
(e) between the heir and the inheritance, which has been accepted with benefit of inventory;
(f) between persons whose property is subjected by law or judicial provisions to the administration of others and those who exercise such administration, until the account is submitted and finally approved;
(g) between legal persons and their administrators, as long as they hold office, with respect to actions for liability against them;
(h) between a debtor who has fraudulently concealed the existence of the debt and the creditor, until the fraud has been discovered.

Prescription periods are suspended due to the condition of certain persons in the following cases (Article 2942 of the Civil Code):

(a) against non-emancipated minors and interdicts for mental infirmity, for the period during which they lack a legal representative and for six months following the appointment of such representative or the termination of the incapacity;
(b) in time of war, against members of the armed forces of the State, whether regular or temporary, and against those who by reason of their office are attached to such armed forces, for the time indicated by the provisions of the wartime laws.

Japan

There are in Japanese statutory law provisions on suspension of time bar (Civil Code, ss. 158–161).

Korea

There are statutory provisions on suspension that only relate to prescription period. The prescription period may in certain circumstances be suspended. The Civil Code so provides:

(a) If a person under disability has no legal representative in the last six months of the prescription period, the prescription period shall not be extinguished until after the lapse of six months from the time when he becomes a person of full capacity or a legal representative assumes office (Article 179 of the Civil Code).
(b) In respect of the rights of a person under disability against his father, mother or his guardian who manages his property, the prescription period shall not be extinguished until after the lapse of six months from the time when he becomes a person of full capacity or a succeeding legal representative assumes office. In

respect of the rights of one spouse to the other, the prescription period shall not be extinguished until after the lapse of six months from the time of dissolution of the marriage (Article 180 of the Civil Code).

(c) In respect of the rights to the estate of inheritance, the prescription period shall not be extinguished until after the lapse of six months from the time of selection of successor, appointment of administrator or adjudication of bankruptcy (Article 181 of the Civil Code).

(d) In case it is impossible to interrupt the prescription period because of *force majeure* or an act of God, the prescription period shall not be extinguished until after the lapse of one month from the time when such interference ceases to exist.

Malta

The causes of suspension of prescription are the following:

(a) by reason of the person of the owner or creditor
General Civil law rule: Prescription does not run against minors and persons interdicted, save as otherwise provided by law (section 2124(1) of the Civil Code. Moreover, by section 2159 of the Civil Code, extinctive prescriptions, except that of 30 years, do not run against minors and persons interdicted.
Rule in commercial matters: Unless the law expressly provides otherwise, the prescriptions established in the Commercial Code shall run against minors and persons interdicted, saving their right of relief against the tutor or curator (section 546 of the Commercial Code).

(b) by the nature of the relationship
Prescription does not run (section 2123 of the Civil Code):

(i) as between spouses;
(ii) as between the father and the child subject to paternal authority;
(iii) as between the person under tutorship or curatorship and his tutor or curator until the tutorship or curatorship ceases, and the accounts are definitely rendered and approved;
(iv) as between the heir and the inheritance entered upon inventory.

Nor does prescription run, during the continuance of the marriage, against a married woman, in any case in which the action competent to the wife, if exercised, would vest the defendant with a right to relief against the husband (section 2124(2) of the Civil Code).

(c) by reason of the modality of the right
Prescription is suspended (section 2125 of the Civil Code):
(i) in regard to conditional rights, until the condition is fulfilled;
(ii) in regard to any other action the exercise of which is suspended for a specified time, until such time expires;
(iii) in regard to actions for breach of warranty, until eviction takes place.

Netherlands

There are no statutory provisions in respect of the suspension of time-bar or extinction periods.

Portugal

The prescription is suspended (Article 321, Nos. 1 and 2 of the Civil Code), during the last three months of the term, if the holder of the right is unable to enforce it owing to an Act of God, or if he does not enforce it as a consequence of deceit of the obligor.

Spain

Both groups of rules of prescription, i.e. the Civil Code and the Commercial Code groups, contemplate only interruption of the time-bar periods. Interruption is distinct from suspension. The former means that a complete period commences to run anew from the date of interruption. Instead, suspension does not delete the time already elapsed. It only stops the running of time. So time continues to run once the period of suspension is finished.

However, it may be said that there is a period of suspension established in the special law on salvage (see page 131, above).

Sweden

The general rule in Swedish law is that there are no general statutory provisions according to which time limits are automatically suspended. Exceptions are found in CMR[8] and COTIF.[9]

Switzerland

The statute of limitations does not start to run, and is suspended in case it has started (Article 134 of the Code of Obligations):

8. Convention on the International Carriage of Goods by Road, 1956.
9. Convention concerning International Carriage by Rail, 1980.

(a) for claims of children against their parents for the duration of the parental power;
(b) for claims of wards against their guardians and the authorities of guardianship for the duration of the guardianship;
(c) for claims of spouses against each other for the duration of the marriage.

The running of the Statute of Limitations is interrupted (Article 135 of the Code of Obligations):

(a) by acknowledgement of the claim by the obligor, in particular also by making interest and installment payments, by giving a pledge or mortgage, or by giving a guarantee;
(b) by prosecution for debt (under the Law on Debt Enforcement and Bankruptcy), or by bringing suit or by raising a defence in court or in arbitration, as well as by filing a claim in a bankruptcy, or by a summons to appear in an official conciliation proceeding.

Turkey

In the Code of Obligations, there is a specific provision on the suspension of the prescription period (Article 132, paragraphs 1–6). This provision does not apply to the extinction periods.

According to this rule, the prescription period is suspended in the following cases:

(a) claims of children against their parents during the course of protection;
(b) claims of persons against the curator and the court of the first instance in the course of curatorship;
(c) claims between spouses;
(d) claims of employees against employment during the contract of employment;
(e) claims on which the debtor benefits from usufruct;
(f) claims that cannot be sued before a Turkish court.

The prescription period begins at the end of the day on which the cause of suspension ceases to exist.

United Kingdom

There are no statutory provisions in respect of suspending the time limit. Once time has begun to run it continues to do so.[10]

10. *Rhodes* v. *Smethurst* (1838) 4 M. & W.

Extension of the limitation period is allowed by statute in prescribed circumstances: see Part II of the Limitation Act 1980. In a nutshell, these are as follows:

(a) Where the plaintiff was under a disability (i.e. infancy or unsoundness of mind) when the action accrued; in this case time starts to run when he ceased to be under a disability (Limitation Act 1980, ss. 28 and 28A).

(b) In cases concerning land, time begins to run from the date when

   (i) the person in possession acknowledges the title of the plaintiff; or

   (ii) a payment has been made in respect of a mortgage debt.

   In other cases, when the person liable acknowledges a debt or any other liquidated claim or makes payment in respect of it (Limitation Act 1980, ss. 29, 30 and 31).

(c) When an action is based on fraud, or is for relief from the consequences of a mistake, or the right of action has been deliberately concealed from the plaintiff, time begins to run from the date the plaintiff discovers the fraud, concealment or mistake or could have discovered it with reasonable diligence (Limitation Act 1980, s. 32).

(d) In actions for libel or slander, the court has discretion to give leave to the plaintiff to bring an action outside the three-year time limit if he does so within one year from the date he knew of all the relevant facts (Limitation Act 1980, s. 32A).

(e) In personal injury actions, the court has discretion not to apply the limitation period (Limitation Act 1980, s. 33).

United States

There are no statutory provisions in respect of suspending the time limit.

Venezuela

Pursuant to Article 1964 of the Civil Code, prescription is suspended:

(a) between spouses;

(b) between the person who exercises paternal authority and the person subject thereto;

(c) between the guardian and the minor or interdict subject to guardianship until guardianship has not terminated and the final accounting has been rendered and approved;

(d) between the curator and the emancipated minor or other disabled person;

(e) between the heir and the inheritance, which has been accepted with benefit of inventory;
(f) between persons who by law are subject to the administration of others and such other persons.

Pursuant to Article 1965 of the Civil code prescription is also suspended:

(a) against the non-emancipated minors and interdicts;
(b) against the rights subject to conditions, until such conditions exist;
(c) against the assets of the husband subject to hypothèque as security for the fulfilment of matrimonial stipulations;
(d) as respects any other action the enforcement of which is suspended;
(e) as respects actions of restitution until eviction has not occurred.

2. WHETHER THE PARTIES MAY AGREE ON THE SUSPENSION OF THE TIME-BAR PERIOD AND, IF SO, HOW

Argentina

It is possible to waive the defence of time bar for the period already elapsed, but not for the future.

Australia

The parties may so agree, but the agreement is only binding if the claimant gives the defendant consideration (that is, something of value, or the promise of something of value) in return for the promise not to rely on the time bar, or if the defendant unequivocally represents that he or she will not rely on the time bar and the claimant detrimentally alters his or her position in reliance on that representation.

Belgium

The prescription period may be interrupted by agreement between the parties, provided, however, such agreement is entered into after the cause of action has arisen (Article 2220 of the Civil Code).

Canada

Parties may agree on the suspension of a time bar. It is questionable whether parties can agree on suspension of an extinction period other than possibly by renouncing the benefit of time already elapsed.

China

There are no provisions in this respect.

Croatia

In maritime law, once the claim has arisen, the parties may extend the time-bar period by written agreement (Article 679 paragraphs 3 and 4 for contract for the employment of ships; Article 764, paragraph 3 for salvage). The debtor may interrupt the time-bar period not only by recognizing the debt to the creditor but indirectly by payment of instalments, by payment of interest and by providing securities to the creditor (Article 387 of the Law of Obligations 1978).

Denmark

The parties may agree on both the suspension and extinction.

Finland

The time limit may be suspended by agreement between the parties.

France

Article 2220 of the Civil Code provides that it is possible to waive the prescription once matured. This gives rise to the generally accepted rule that the parties may by agreement suspend the prescription that has recommenced to run.

Germany

The parties are allowed to alleviate the time bar, that means to shorten the period. Apart from this the time bar is suspended as long as the parties agree the payment to be deferred.

Greece

A prescription period cannot be suspended by agreement between the parties.

India

A prescription period cannot be suspended by agreement between the parties.

Ireland

An agreement between the parties that the time bar will not be pleaded is binding.

Israel

The Limitation Act allows to extend the period of limitation by agreement, but the agreement must be in writing and in a separate contract.

Italy

Prescription is of public order. The statutory provisions on the periods of prescription, its suspension or interruption are, therefore, compulsory. Article 2936 of the Civil Code provides that any agreement aiming at modifying the statutory regime of the prescription is null and void. Article 2937 in turn provides that prescription can be waived only after it has matured.

These rules, as previously stated, do not apply to the extinction periods qualified in Italian law as *decadenza* (*déchéance*) and in respect of such latter periods suspension, extension or waiver are not prohibited. In this respect the qualification of the one-year time limit of the Hague-Visby Rules as a *decadenza* by the Italian Supreme Court is relevant since it has allowed Italian courts to state that an extension of the one-year time limit is valid and binding upon the carrier.

Japan

It is not permissible to interrupt or suspend a prescription period by an agreement between the parties or to waive the benefit of prescription in advance (Civil Code, s. 146) with the exception that the period mentioned at page 88 may be extended by an agreement made between the parties after the occurrence of the damage to or loss of cargo (International Carriage of Goods by Sea Act, s. 14). But this provision is interpreted so that a party may waive the benefit of prescription for the period which has elapsed.

Korea

The statutory provisions on the period of prescription are compulsory. It is not permissible to suspend the period by an agreement between the parties or to waive the benefit of the period in advance. However, it may be shortened or lessened and the benefit of the prescription period can be waived only after it has matured (Article 184 of the Civil Code).

There are no statutory provisions on the suspension of extinction periods in general. However, where there are special provisions, they may be extended by an agreement between the parties (Article 811, 812–816, 842, 848 and 860 of the Commercial Code).

Malta

The only causes which suspend prescription are those contained in sections 2123–2125 mentioned above at pages 163–164 above. Prescription cannot be renounced beforehand, nor is it lawful to establish a time for prescription longer than that specified by law (section 2108 of the Civil Code). Prescription already acquired may be renounced.

Mexico

Prescription may be suspended by agreement between the parties.

Netherlands

A time bar or extinction period as provided for by Book 8 of the Civil Code (Law of Carriage) may be extended by a contract between parties, after the fact causing the action has occurred (Civil Code, Art. 8:1701).

A time-bar or extinction period according to general law (Book 3 of the Civil Code) cannot be extended.

Norway

When the claim has arisen, the debtor may agree to an extension of the limitation period. However, pursuant to Article 28 of the Act of 18 May 1979, no. 18 (Limitation Act) the agreement cannot be given effect for more than three years, calculated from the date of the agreement.

Example. An agreement made one year before the expiration of the limitation period cannot extend the period by more than two years: one + two = three years, and the agreement cannot be given effect more than three years after its conclusion.

Successive agreements for extension cannot, pursuant to Article 28 referred to above, extend the original period by more than 10 years. The limitation period for maritime liens cannot be prolonged by an agreement between the parties.

Poland

The parties may not agree to suspend the time-bar period.

Portugal

Pursuant to Article 300 of the Civil Code, all covenants aiming at modifying the statutory prescription and legal time limits are null and void.

The periods of *caducidade*,[11] generally are not suspended or interrupted (Article 328 of the Civil Code). However, according to Article 33, No. 1 of the Civil Code, agreements by which special cases of *caducidade* are created, the legal regime of *caducidade* is modified or renounced are valid, as long as they are not against the will of the parties or are in fraud to the legal rules for prescription.

Russia

Under Russian legislation the agreement between the parties concerning the suspension or the interruption of a time-bar period is null and void and of no effect with the exception of the cases when the possibility of agreement is expressly stipulated by any international treaty, to which Russia is a party.

Spain

Extinctive prescription has a public order character. Therefore, Article 1935 of the Civil Code bans any waiver of the prescription made in advance. Any agreement aiming at modifying the statutory regime of the prescription is null and void. However, the same Article 1935 of the Civil Code allows the waiver of the prescription once it has matured.

Sweden

The parties are able to agree upon a prolongation of the time bar according to the Swedish Maritime Code, maximum three years at a time and never more than 10 years in total. This, however, is not the case according to the general code on time limits. In the latter case the running of a time bar may be stopped simply through the act of presenting the debtor with a claim. It therefore becomes unnecessary to prescribe that the parties may reach an agreement on extension of time.

Switzerland

Usually when parties wish to agree on an extension of time after the claim has already accrued and the time of the prescription period has started to run, the parties will waive their rights under applicable Statutes of Limitations and in particular waive the possibility to plead lapse of time in a subsequent court proceeding (*Verjährungsverzichtserklärung*).

11. See page 6 above.

Turkey

The parties are allowed to extend the period of limitation by agreement except in respect of commercial cases (Article 6 of the Turkish Code).

United Kingdom

Parties may agree on a suspension of time limit. This may be done by an express agreement[12] by waiver[13] or by estoppel.[14]

United States

The parties may enter an agreement which extends the statute of limitations provided the agreement is reasonable. If the agreement is only oral, it must be supported by some sort of consideration.[15]

3. WHETHER THE TIME BAR MAY BE EXTENDED BY THE COURT

Argentina

No. Prescription cannot be extended by a court at its discretion.

Australia

1. In New South Wales, Victoria, Queensland, Tasmania and the Northern Territory:

—Where the action is based upon the fraud of the defendant or his or her agent, or of any person through whom the plaintiff claims (or his or her agent), or where the right of action is concealed by the fraud of any of these people, the time-bar period begins from the date when the fraud has been discovered or, with reasonable diligence, might have been discovered.[16]

2. In Northern Territory and South Australia:

—Any of the limitation periods described above may be extended on application to the court.[17]

12. *Lubovsky* v. *Snelling* [1944] KB 44.
13. *Kammins Ballrooms Co.* v. *Zenith Investments Ltd.* [1971] AC 850.
14. *Patterson* v. *Glasgow Corporation* (1908) 46 SLR 10.
15. 54 Corpus Juris Secundum, para. 23.
16. Limitation Act 1969 (NSW), s. 55; Limitation of Actions Act 1958 (Vic), s. 27; Limitation of Actions Act 1974 (Qld), s. 38; Limitation Act 1974 (Tas), s. 32 and Limitation Act 1981 (NT), s. 42).
17. Limitation of Actions Act 1936 (SA), s. 48; Limitation Act 1981 (NT), s. 44).

3. In New South Wales, Tasmania and the Northern Territory:

—The court may extend the limitation period for a claim for damage done by a ship, or a claim for salvage services to a ship, if it is satisfied that there has not, during the limitation period, been a reasonable opportunity for arresting the ship within the jurisdiction of the court or within the territorial waters of the country to which the plaintiff's vessel belongs or in which the plaintiff resides or has his or her principal place of business. The court may extend the limitation period to an extent sufficient to give a reasonable opportunity of arresting the ship.[18]

4. In every jurisdiction except Western Australia:

—The court may, on application to it, extend the time-bar period for commencement of an action in respect of personal injuries.[19]

5. In Western Australia:

—The court may only extend the time-bar period in respect of personal injuries arising out of the inhalation of asbestos.[20]

Belgium

The prescription cannot be extended by the court.

China

No. A court may not extend the time-bar period at its discretion.

Croatia

No. A court may not extend the time-bar period at its discretion.

France

No. Prescription cannot be extended by a court at its discretion.

Greece

No. Prescription cannot be extended by a court at its discretion.

18. Limitation Act 1969 (NSW), s. 22(4); Limitation Act 1974 (Tas), s. 8(4) and Limitation Act 1981 (NT), s. 20(5).

19. Limitation Act 1969 (NSW), ss. 57, 58; Limitation of Actions Act 1958 (Vic), s. 23A; Limitation of Actions Act 1974 (Qld), ss. 30—4; Limitation of Actions Act 1936 (SA), s. 48 (general extension provision); Limitation Act 1974 (Tas), s. 5(3) and Limitation Act 1981 (NT), s. 44 (general extension provision).

20. Limitation Act 1935 (WA), s. 38A.

Italy

No. Prescription cannot be extended by a court at its discretion.

Japan

No. Prescription cannot be extended by a court at its discretion.

Netherlands

The time-bar period cannot be extended by the court.

Norway

Time limits cannot be extended by a court at its discretion.

Poland

No. Prescription cannot be extended by the court.

Spain

The court itself has no power to extend the period of extinctive prescription. This has to be done by the debtor, by way of waiver, as explained supra in paragraph 2 (see Article 942 of the Commercial Code).

Sweden

Time limits cannot be extended by a court at its discretion.

Switzerland

It does not lie within the discretion of the court to extend the time bar. The extensions of time granted by the court are merely procedural time limits and therefore only relate to procedural steps within the court proceedings. However, every court action (as a court hearing or order) regarding the claim pending before the court will, as such, interrupt the prescription period.

Turkey

No. Time limits cannot be extended by the court.

4. STATUTORY RULES ON THE INTERRUPTION OF THE TIME-BAR PERIODS

(i) INTERRUPTION BY COMMENCEMENT OF A JUDICIAL PROCEEDING—WHEN THE PROCEEDING IS DEEMED TO BE COMMENCED

Argentina

The prescription period may be interrupted by a judicial action and the proceeding must be commenced before the expiration of the time limit.

As regards suspension of the prescription period, Article 3986 of the Civil Code provides:

Prescription is interrupted by an action against the person in possession, even if commenced before a judge without jurisdiction, or, if annulled due to a formal defect or because the plaintiff did not have the legal capacity to be a party in the judicial proceedings.
The prescription period may be suspended only once by claiming payment to the debtor through any authentic means. Such suspension will only have effect during the term of one year or during the shortest term corresponding to the prescription of the action (Article 3986).

There has been a long discussion about the application of this provision of the Civil Code to commercial claims. There is now a decision of the Supreme Court holding that Article 3986 of the Civil Code is applicable to commercial claims and the same construction is applicable to maritime claims.

Belgium

The prescription period is interrupted by commencement of a judicial action (Article 2244 of the Civil Code).

Brazil

The prescription period is interrupted by the commencement of judicial proceedings (Article 172 of the Commercial Code).

Canada

The running of the time limit is interrupted by the proper commencement of a valid judicial proceeding once issued by the court, provided such proceedings are served within the time provided under the relevant court rules.

Chile

The formal interruption of prescription is produced by a "judicial complaint". The Chilean legal writers and jurisprudence have conflicting views with respect to the moment when the interruption of the prescription is effective. The most widely accepted view is that the interruption is produced by the service of the claim to the debtor or obligor. According to another view the filing of the claim in Court is sufficient to produce the interruption.

China

The institution of a lawsuit interrupts the running of the time-bar period (Article 26 of the Maritime Law) and the time of instituting such lawsuit is regarded as the time of the suspension of the time-bar period. The time of instituting such lawsuit is usually determined by the time when the bill of complaint is submitted. Once the time-bar period is interrupted, it commences to run again from the date of interruption.

Croatia

The running of time-bar period may be interrupted by commencement of judicial proceedings, i.e. when the action has been brought before the court.

Denmark

General interruption is effected by commencement of judicial proceedings, which is deemed to be commenced as of the date when the competent court has received a writ of summons, or in case of arbitration agreement, initiating arbitration, see page 195 below.

Finland

The limits are interrupted by the commencement of judicial proceedings.

France

Prescription is interrupted by commencement of judicial proceedings (Article 2244 of the Civil Code). Normally it is the service by a court bailiff of the writ of summons to the defendant that causes the interruption. However, in the exceptional cases where the action is commenced before the Tribunal de Grande Instance (for example, by a passenger) and not before the Tribunal de Commerce, the writ of summons, in order that it may maintain all its effects, must be filed at the Tribunal within four months. If it is not filed, it loses its value. The interruption continues to have effect until the final decision of the judges.

Germany

The judicial proceedings commence by service of process.

Greece

Pursuant to Article 261 of the Civil Code, a prescription period is interrupted by bringing an action.

India

The commencement of judicial proceedings interrupts the running of the time bar.

Ireland

The commencement of a judicial proceeding interrupts the running of the time bar. The date of commencement of proceedings is the date of issue of the originating summons by the Central Office of the High Court.

Israel

The limitation period is interrupted by instituting an action in court.

Japan

Prescription is interrupted *inter alia* by a demand (*Sikyu*) from an obligee (Civil Code, s. 147).

The demand includes the following:

(a) Demand by way of judicial proceedings (Civil Code, ss. 149, and 150).

(b) Summons from a court for compromise or voluntary appearance of an obligee for the same purpose before a court (Civil Code, s. 151).

(c) Intervention in bankruptcy proceedings (Civil Code, s. 152), composition proceedings (Composition Act, supplementary provisions, para. 2), corporate reorganization proceedings (Corporate Reorganization Act, s. 5) or shipowner's liability limitation proceedings (Act for Limitation of Liability of Shipowners, s. 54) and,

(iv) Peremptory notice.

The interruption by the demand by way of judicial proceedings becomes effective at the time of the petition being submitted to a court (Civil Procedure Act, s. 235).

A prescription period commences to run anew from the day on which the cause of interruption of such a period ceases to exist. A prescription period interrupted by a court procedure commences to run anew from the day on which the judgment thereon becomes finally binding (Civil Code, s. 157). The period of prescription in respect of rights established by judgments which have become finally binding is 10 years, even as regards those for which a period shorter than 10 years is provided for under the law. The same shall also apply to a right established by judicial compromise, judicial conciliation or any other process having the same effect as judgments which have become finally binding; provided, however, that this period of prescription shall not apply to claims which are not yet due at the time when they are established (Civil Code, s. 174–2).

Korea

The interruption of prescription by means of a judicial claim takes effect at the time when the suit has been filed by a claimant with a court or when the document has been submitted to the court in case of an amendment of the claim or the suit for the interlocutory confirmation of the establishment of a legal relation (Article 238 of the Code of Civil Procedure).

Malta

Prescription is interrupted by a judicial demand that must have for its object the exercise of the action which is in danger of being prescribed. It must be served on the defendant personally or on his representative. An interruption by means of a judicial demand is perfected by the judgment given upon the demand—thus, the interruption is inoperative if the plaintiff withdraws his demand, or if the action is deserted, or is dismissed.

The interruption of prescription against one of the heirs of one of the joint and several debtors, shall not be operative against the other codebtors except with regard to the part of the debt for which such heir is liable (section 1101(2)). Nevertheless, where prescription has been interrupted against all the heirs of the deceased co-debtor, such interruption shall be operative against all the surviving co-debtors for the whole debt (section 1101(3)). An act which interrupts prescription as against the debtor is effectual as an interruption against the surety. Where the surety has bound himself jointly and severally with the principal debtor, the provisions of sections 1100 and 1101 above mentioned shall apply.

Mexico

Prescription is interrupted by court proceedings.

Netherlands

A time-bar period can be interrupted, an extinction period cannot. The time bar of a right of action to claim performance of an obligation is interrupted by:

(a) The institution of an action (Civil Code, Art. 3:315). For example: the issuing of a writ of summons. A judicial proceeding is deemed to be commenced by the issuing of a writ of summons.
(b) Any other act of judicial recourse instituted in the required form. For example, attachment (Civil Code, Art. 3:316).
(c) An act to obtain a binding opinion, provided that the other party is expeditiously notified of it and that a binding opinion actually results (Civil Code, Art. 3:316).
(d) A written warning or a written communication in which the creditor unequivocally reserves his right to performance (Civil Code, Art. 3:317).
(e) Acknowledgement of the creditor's right (Civil Code, Art. 3:318).

The time bar of other rights of action is interrupted by:

(a) The institution of an action (Civil Code, Art. 3:316).
(b) Any other act of judicial recourse instituted in the required form (Civil Code, Art. 3:316).
(c) An act to obtain a binding opinion, provided that the other party is expeditiously notified of it and that a binding opinion actually results (Civil Code, Art. 3:316).
(d) A written warning followed within six months by an act of interruption as described under (a), (b) and (c) (Civil Code, Art. 3:317).
(e) Acknowledgement of the creditor's right (Civil Code, Art. 3:318).

"A right of action to claim performance of an obligation" is, for example, the right of action to claim freight. It is not certain whether the right of action to claim compensation for damage (i.e. a cargo claim) comes under "a right of action to claim performance of an obligation" or under "other rights of action". This is of importance in the event of the action having been interrupted by a written warning. If the right of action to claim compensation for damage comes under "other rights of action", interruption occurs only if the written warning is followed within six months by an act of interruption as described under (a), (b) and (c) above. So long as this question has not been answered by the jurisprudence, it would be safer to assume that this kind of action comes under "other rights of action".

The interruption of the time bar of a right of action otherwise than by the institution of an action which is upheld, starts a new time-bar period as of the beginning of the following day (Civil Code, Art. 3:319).

The power to execute forceably a judicial or arbitral decision is time-barred by 20 years from the beginning of the day following the decision. Payments to be made annually or more frequently pursuant to the decision are time-barred by five years (Civil Code, Art. 3:324).

Norway

Proceedings are deemed to be commenced from the date when the summons to the appropriate court is put in the mail. It is, of course, advisable to secure evidence by using registered mail or a copy of the envelope with the post-office stamp, etc.

Poland

The running of the time-bar period is interrupted by the commencement of judicial proceedings.

In the case of an interruption to the prescription by proceedings before a court of law or other authority entitled to decide cases or enforce claims of a given type or before a court of arbitration, the prescription period does not start anew until the proceeding has come to an end.

Portugal

Prescription is interrupted by service of process (Articles 323, 324 and 325 of the Civil Code).

Russia

The time-bar period is interrupted by the commencement of judicial proceedings.

Spain

General statutory provisions in respect of interruption of the prescription are contained in Article 1973 of the Civil Code.

Special rules for interruption of contractual commercial obligations and for collision, are specified in Article 944 of the Commercial Code.

Besides, special rules provided in maritime international conventions have to be taken into account.

In the Civil Code regime any act by which the action is exercised in a judicial proceeding interrupts prescription (Article 1973). A claim made to the judge suffices. Proceeding is deemed to be commenced not only with the formal commencement of a lawsuit. Requesting to the judge a simple act of conciliation will suffice.

The Commercial Code seems to establish a very similar regime. Prescription is interrupted by commencement of a lawsuit or by any other kind of judicial claim made to the debtor. However, interruption does not occur if the suit is not admitted, if the plaintiff discontinues the action or if the proceeding is extinguished pursuant to the rules of Procedural Law (see Article 944 of the Commercial Code and Articles 411 *et seq.* of the Ley de Enjuiciamiento Civil).

Sweden

The proceedings are considered to have been initiated at such time when the court receives the application to sue.

Switzerland

The commencement of action interrupting time bar means the initial or preparatory action of the claimant provided by Cantonal law, by which the claimant invokes formally the protection of the judge for his claim, for the first time.

The time bar is also interrupted by a party submitting an objection in a pending court proceeding according to the formalities of the Cantonal law.

Turkey

The time-bar periods (prescription and extinction periods) are interrupted by commencement of judicial proceedings. The proceeding is deemed to commence by instituting an action in court or arbitral tribunal (Article 133 of the Code of Obligations).

United Kingdom

Once a plaintiff has commenced judicial proceedings, time stops running. Proceedings are commenced by the issuing of a writ or other originating process, e.g. originating summons. Time stops running at the date of the issue of process. Order 6, Rule 7(3) of the Rules of the Supreme Court provides that the issue of a writ takes place upon its being sealed by the Court.

United States

The commencement of a judicial proceeding suspends the statute of limitations. A proceeding is deemed commenced when the complaint is filed, Federal Rules of Civil Procedure, Rule 3. However, in diversity cases, state statutes are applied, and in some states proceedings do not commence until process has been served on the opposing party.

Venezuela

Prescription is interrupted by the serving of a summons to the debtor and the court issuing to the debtor an order to enter an appearance, provided the claimant does not discontinue the proceedings (Article 1969, 1972 and 1973 of the Civil Code).

(ii) INTERRUPTION BY OTHER TYPES OF ACTION

Brazil

Prescription is interrupted by any judicial act which puts the debtor on notice.

Canada

No. These other types of action are considered incidental proceedings to a principal action.

Chile

Article 1250 of the Commercial Code allows the repeated, voluntary interruption of the time limit by means of written statements of the claimant. The time commences to run from the date of the last interruption.

China

The Civil Procedure Law of the People's Republic of China has no special stipulations in this regard. In this law, the stipulations on security measures in respect of property widely differ from the stipulations on "injunction" and "arrest or attachment of a property of the debtor" in force in other countries.

However, the application by the claimant for the arrest of a vessel may interrupt the time-bar period, as provided in Article 267 of the Maritime Law, and the time when the application is filed is regarded as the time of such interruption. Application by the parties concerned for taking security measures may possibly interrupt the time-bar period, though there are no explicit provisions in the laws.

Croatia

The running of the time-bar period may be interrupted by any other action of the creditor against the debtor before the court such as filing the petition in a bankruptcy proceeding or other competent authority in order to establish, secure or enforce the claim (Article 388 of the Law of Obligations).

Denmark

In the case of maritime liens, interruption is effected only if an arrest or an execution by the bailiff's court is made. These actions are probably deemed to be commenced at the date when the request is received by the competent court, or at least when the arrest order is issued.

France

Prescription is equally interrupted by commencement of the proceedings *en référé* (Article 2244 of the Civil Code, as amended by Law 5 July 1985). But distinctions must be made:

(a) Commencement of proceedings *en référé* for the appointment of an expert interrupts the prescription. But a new prescription period of the same length as the previous one (for example, one year for the carriage of goods) commences to run again from the date when the judge appoints the expert.
(b) Commencement of the proceedings *en référé* with a view to obtaining a payment on account (Article 809 of the Nouveau Code de Procedure Civile) equally interrupts the prescription. But it is the general prescription (10 years; Article 189 *bis* of the Code de Commerce) that commences to run again once the order for a payment on account is issued. In conformity with the general rule, the interruption of the main action cannot be extended to the cross action.
(c) On the other hand, neither an intimation of payment, even by means of court bailiff, nor the arrest of the ship, or of other assets of the debtor, interrupts the prescription. A particular case is that of the interruption of the prescription in respect of maritime liens. In the absence of statutory provisions, the question is in dispute. Since the subject matter of the maritime lien is only the ship, it would appear that only the arrest of the

ship may interrupt the prescription of the maritime lien on such ship.

Germany

There are different types of action that may interrupt the running of the time, for example by application of judicial reminder for payment of a debt (*Mahnbescheid*) or by filing of a maritime claim for distribution of a limitation fund.

Greece

Pursuant to Articles 264 and 269 of the Civil Code, a prescription period is interrupted by the serving of an enforceable judgment or other enforceable document and by the filing of a claim in bankruptcy proceedings or in the procedure of forced sale.

Italy

Yes. A conserving arrest or a seizure has the effect, pursuant to Article 2943 of the Civil Code, of interrupting the prescription.

Japan

As stated at page 177 above, a demand, whereby prescription may be interrupted, includes:

(a) Summons from a court for compromise, or voluntary appearance of an obligee for the same purpose before a court (Civil Code, s. 151).

(b) Intervention in bankruptcy proceedings (Civil Code, s. 152), composition proceedings (Composition Act, supplementary provisions, para. 2), corporate reorganization proceedings (Corporate Reorganization Act, s. 5) or shipowner's liability limitation proceedings (Act for Limitation of Liability of Shipowners, s. 54).

Korea

The prescription period is interrupted by other types of action. The Civil Code provides:

(a) *Intervention in bankruptcy*: it shall not, however, have the effect of interrupting prescription periods, if it is withdrawn by the creditor or if his claim is dismissed (Article 171 of the Civil Code).

(b) *Order for payment*: it shall not, however, have the effect of interrupting prescription, if it lapses due to the claimant's failure to apply for provisional execution within the period of time prescribed by law (Article 172 of the Civil Code).

(c) *Summons for compromise or voluntary appearance for the same purpose*: summons for compromise shall not have the effect of interrupting prescription, unless an action is brought by one of the parties within one month, in cases when the other party does not appear or the compromise is not concluded. The same shall apply to the voluntary appearance, if a compromise has not been concluded (Article 173 of the Civil Code).

Attachment, provisional attachment, provisional disposition shall not, however, have the effect of interrupting prescription, if cancelled by the request of the claimant or by reason of non-compliance with a provision of law (Article 175 of the Civil Code). Also, they shall not be effective if the beneficiary of the prescription has not been notified thereof (Article 176 of the Civil Code).

Netherlands

The other types of action whereby time-bar periods can be interrupted are set out on page 179.

Norway

All such actions require the issue of an originating summons. Accordingly, proceedings are deemed to be commenced from the date when the summons to the appropriate court is put in the mail. It is, of course, advisable to secure evidence by using registered mail or a copy of the envelope with the post-office stamp, etc.

Spain

Prescription is interrupted by any kind of judicial action of the many types established in Spanish procedural law, including any arrest or seizure against the vessel or the property of the debtor.

Switzerland

Injunctions and arrests do not affect the time running under a prescription period. In order to interrupt the prescription period, the attachment of the debtor's property is not necessary, since the summons (payment order) already issued by the debt collection office will interrupt the prescription period.

Turkey

The time-bar periods are interrupted either by referring to the Court Bailiff's Office or to the Board of Bankruptcy (Article 133 of the Code of Obligations).

United Kingdom

In all circumstances, whether applying for summary judgment, an injunction, or the arrest or attachment of the debtor's property, the time bar may only be interrupted by the issuing of an originating process.

United States

If there is an injunction against bringing the suit it suspends the Statute of limitations for that suit.[21]

(iii) INTERRUPTION BY A NOTICE OF DEFAULT OR FORMAL REQUEST OF PAYMENT

Belgium

No. Prescription cannot be interrupted by a notice of default.

Canada

No. Time-bar cannot be interrupted by a notice of default.

China

The time-bar period cannot be interrupted by a notice of default or formal request for payment. However, the Maritime Code provides in Article 267 that agreement by the person against whom the legal proceedings are instituted to fulfil his obligations may interrupt the time-bar period, and the time when he agrees to do so shall be taken as the time of such interruption. But where the limitation of action as provided in the General Principles of Civil Law is applicable, it would appear that there are also grounds to invoke the provisions in the above law as regards the interruption of the time-bar period. However, Article 140 of the General Principles of Civil Law provides that the time-bar period is interrupted if suit is brought or if one party makes a claim for, or agrees to the fulfillment of, his obligations. A new limitation period shall count from the time of the interruption.

21. West's Federal Digest 4th, Limitation of Actions, s. 135.

Croatia

The running period is not interrupted by a notice of default or formal request by the creditor to the debtor (Article 391 of the Law of Obligations 1978).

Denmark

In cases of defective goods, interruption of the one-year time limit according to the Sales of Goods Act, s. 54, is effected by notifying the Seller.

France

No. Prescription may not be interrupted by a notice of default.

Germany

Prescription may not be interrupted by a notice of default.

Greece

A prescription period cannot be interrupted by a notice of default or a formal request of payment.

Ireland

Time is not interrupted merely by the presentation of a Notice of Default or formal request of payment. A reminder sent by the creditor to the debtor about the claim does not stop the time-bar period from running out.

Israel

A reminder to the debtor would not interrupt the limitation period.

Italy

Prescription is interrupted by any act that has the effect of placing the debtor in a situation of default (*Mora* or, in French, *Demeure*), *viz.* by an intimation of payment in writing (Article 2943 of the Civil Code).

Japan

As stated above at pages 177 and 178 a demand includes a "Peremptory notice" whose effect is, therefore, that of interrupting the prescription.

However, the peremptory notice does not have the effect of interruption, unless the demand other than the peremptory notice, attachment, provisional attachment or provisional disposition, are taken within six months (Civil Code, s. 153).

Korea

A reminder has the effect of interrupting the prescription period, if an action, a summons or compromise, or a voluntary appearance for the same purpose, intervention in bankruptcy proceedings, an attachment, a provisional attachment or a disposition, is taken within six months (Article 174 of the Civil Code).

Malta

Time limits in the Commercial Code are periods of forfeiture and may thus not be interrupted by the usual methods of interruption, e.g. judicial letters. The time limits in the Civil Code may be interrupted by a natural or civil cause. A natural cause is only applicable to acquisitive prescription where section 2127 of the Civil Code provides that prescription is interrupted when the possessor is deprived, for more than one year, of the enjoyment of the thing, whether by the owner or by a third party.

Civil interruption may be brought about by a judicial act made either by the owner or creditor. The act of the owner or creditor may be either a judicial act or a judicial demand purporting to assert the right that is in danger of being prescribed. The judicial act is a protest or a judicial letter, filed in the name of the owner or of the creditor, and served on the party against whom it is sought to prevent the running of prescription or on his lawful representative (section 2128). It must be filed before the completion of prescription, but it is operative if served before the expiration of one month, to be reckoned from the last day of the period of prescription (section 2130(1)). If the party to be served is absent from Malta, service shall be deemed to be effected by the publication of a notice in the Government Gazette, within one month, commencing from the last day of the aforesaid period, on the demand of the party filing the act, as provided in the Code of Civil Procedure (section 2130(2)). Although interruption is inoperative if the act is null owing to a defect in its substance. It is, however, operative even if it is null owing to a defect in its form or being filed before a court, which is not the competent court (section 2129).

Netherlands

Time bars can be interrupted by a written warning as indicated at page 179 above.

Norway

Notice of default or formal request of payment is never sufficient to interrupt a time limit.

Portugal

Prescription is interrupted by any notice which conveys, directly or indirectly, the intention to exercise the right.

Spain

The Civil Code recognizes as well any extrajudicial claim made to the debtor as a cause of interruption of the prescription (Article 1973 of the Civil Code). There are no special requirements as to the form of the claim. Any kind of claim that may be proved will be enough. However, this cause of interruption is not recognized in the Commercial Code and therefore, is not applicable to collision and to the main maritime contractual obligations.

Sweden

According to the General Swedish Statute on time limits an interruption of the time bar/extinction period occurs when the debtor receives notice of the debt. This however is not the case according to Swedish maritime law when legal action is required.

Switzerland

A notice of default is not sufficient; the formal payment order has to be done by a summons (payment order) issued by the debt-collection office at the request of the creditor.

Turkey

The time-bar period is not interrupted merely by a notice of default or formal request of payment.

United Kingdom

The running of time may be interrupted where the debtor acknowledges the debt or makes part payment in respect of the debt. In these circumstances the right of action will accrue on and not before the date of the acknowledgment or payment (Limitation Act 1980, s. 29(5)).

United States

Neither of these actions interrupts a Statute of Limitations.

Venezuela

Prescription is interrupted by any proceedings that constitute the debtor in default. This, however, is not the case for time limits that have the legal nature of *caducidade*,[22] since for these time limits, the only manner to prevent the lapse of time is to bring an action against the debtor.

(iv) OTHER MANNERS OF INTERRUPTION

Belgium

Prescription is interrupted by the acknowledgement of the debt by the debtor (Article 2248 of the Civil Code).

Brazil

Prescription is interrupted by the acknowledgement of the debt by the debtor (Article 172 of the Commercial Code).

China

Except for the stipulations in Article 267 of the Maritime Code and Article 140 of the General Principles of Civil Law, which sets out the circumstances in which the time-bar period may be suspended, the laws have no provisions as to other manners that may suspend the time-bar period.

Finland

A mere notice given by the claimant to the debtor may interrupt the general 10-year time limit, but not the special time limits.

France

Prescription may only be interrupted in the manners set out at pages 176 and 183.

Germany

The running of the time may only be interrupted in the manners set out at pages 177 and 184, above.

22. See page 2 above.

Greece

A prescription period may be interrupted by off-setting the claim in court against a counterclaim.

Ireland

Only the issue of proceedings, the agreement of the parties, acknowledgement, or part payment interrupt the running of the time.

Israel

The limitation period is stopped by acknowledgment from the debtor, made in writing or before a court. The limitation period will start to run afresh from such acknowledgment, even if the original period of limitation has run out before.

India

The running of the time limit is interrupted by the acknowledgement in writing or the partial payment by the debtor.

Italy

Prescription is interrupted by the acknowledgment of the right by the person against whom such right may be enforced (Article 2944 of the Civil Code).

Japan

Prescription may only be interrupted in the manners set out at pages 177, 178 and 184, above.

Korea

Prescription period is interrupted by the acknowledgement of the debtor (Article 168(3) of the Civil Code).

Malta

Civil interruption may be brought about also by an act of the possessor or of the debtor. Such act consists of an acknowledgement of the right of the party against whom prescription has commenced (Civil Code, section 2133). Prescription is interrupted by a payment on account of the debt made by the debtor himself or by a person acting on his behalf (Civil

Code, section 2134). An acknowledgement of the debt by one of the joint and several debtors, and every other act capable of interrupting prescription with regard to any one of such debtors, shall interrupt prescription also with regard to the other debtors and their heirs (Civil Code, section 1100). An acknowledgement of the debt by one of the heirs of one of the joint and several debtors, and every other act executed against such heir, shall not, even though such acknowledgement or act may interrupt prescription with regard to such heir, interrupt prescription with regard to the other co-heirs, even though the debt be a hypothecary debt, unless the obligation be indivisible (Civil Code, section 1101(1)).

Netherlands

Time-bar periods may only be interrupted in the manners set out at pages 179 and 180.

Norway

Only the methods specified in Sections 14–19 of the Limitation Act constitute a valid interruption of the time limit.

Poland

Prescription is interrupted by the acknowledgement of the debt by the debtor. The operation of the prescription is interrupted also by the commencement before the Marine Chamber of proceedings in respect of the collision (Article 235 of the Maritime Code) and by the commencement of adjustment proceedings in respect of general average (Article 229 of the Maritime Code).

Portugal

An implied acknowledgement is relevant, for the purpose of interrupting the prescription, only if it results from facts that express such acknowledgement in an unmistakable manner.

Russia

The acknowledgement of the debt by the debtor has the effect of suspending and not of interrupting the time-bar period.

Spain

In the Civil Code, prescription is also interrupted by any act done by the debtor, whereby the debt is acknowledged (Article 1973 of the Civil

Code). Any act of the debtor from which it may be, directly or indirectly, ascertained that he acknowledges his debt suffices.[23]

In addition, the Commercial Code provides that the interruption is caused by the acknowledgement of the debt by the debtor or by the renewal of the document in which the right of the creditor is founded. In the former case (acknowledgement of the debt) the prescription period commences to run again from the date of the acknowledgement. In the latter case (renewal of document), from the date of the new document. However, should the time for fulfilling the obligation be extended in the new document, then the time counts as of the new date for fulfillment thereby fixed (Article 544 of the Commercial Code).

Sweden

Time limits are interrupted through the acknowledgement by the debtor towards the creditor that the claim in fact exists. A confirmation will be considered to have been given either through the making of a payment by the debtor (capital/interest) or through a simple oral acknowledgement of the existence of debts.

Switzerland

The time-bar may only be interrupted in the manners set out at pages 181 and 185, above.

Turkey

The time-bar period is interrupted where the debtor acknowledges the debt or makes partial payment related to the debt or establishes security for the debt (Article 133 of the Code of Obligations).

United Kingdom

Under the common law, where a creditor has accepted a negotiable instrument as payment for a debt, the cause of action is suspended until the negotiable instrument is dishonoured. Alternatively, the debtor and the creditor may make arrangement for payment to be made in some other way, failing which the creditor can resort to the original cause of action. In these circumstances, time does not begin to run until the default.

United States

When, in conjunction with the legislative scheme, courts will apply the doctrine of equitable tolling of the statute of limitations to avoid technical

23. Judgment of the Tribunal Supremo of 12 March 1970.

forfeitures which would unjustifiably prevent a trial on the merits. For example, this doctrine is used where suit was not brought in a timely manner because of fraudulent concealment of a cause of action, duress or undue influence, or a reasonable mistake on the part of one of the parties.[24]

Venezuela

The acknowledgement of the debt by the debtor interrupts the prescription. The notice given by the claimant to the debtor, if given extra-judicially, interrupts the prescription probably only when the debt is liquid in its amount and payment is due.

5. INTERRUPTION OF THE TIME BAR WHEN THE DISPUTE MUST BE SUBMITTED TO ARBITRATION

Argentina

When the case must be submitted to arbitration, the interruption or the suspension of the prescription period must be done by filing a claim in court or commencing arbitration proceedings in due time.

As the interruption of the prescription period requires a clear intention to keep the action alive, the appointment of the first arbitrator would be sufficient.

Australia

The running of a limitation period is not interrupted by arbitration, in the sense that "interruption" is defined at page 157. Appointment of an arbitrator does not start a new limitation period running, but it may constitute commencement of an action within an existing limitation period if the parties have agreed to submit all disputes to arbitration.

Canada

The time-bar is interrupted by notification of appointment of an arbitrator where the parties have agreed to binding arbitration.

Chile

If the dispute is subject to arbitration the prescription is deemed to be interrupted by the valid judicial service of the claim to the debtor or obligor. There is no jurisprudence on this point and some have held that the

24. 54 Corpus Juris Secundum, paras. 85–86.

prescription is interrupted by serving an application to the Court for the appointment of an arbitrator (in Chile the arbitrator or arbitrators are appointed either by the parties or by the court).

China

Submitting the dispute to arbitration may suspend the time-bar period as provided in Article 267 of the Maritime Code, and the time of submission is taken as the time of suspension. The time of submission is usually determined by the time of filing the application for arbitration, in accordance with the provisions of the arbitration rules.

Croatia

If the dispute must be submitted to arbitration, the running of the time-bar period is interrupted on the date when the action is brought before the permanent arbitration court or in case of ad hoc arbitration, on the date on which the notice of arbitration is received by the respondent.

Denmark

The running of the time-bar period is interrupted by giving notice of appointment of the arbitrator unless the arbitral tribunal is appointed beforehand. In the latter situation interruption is effected by filing the points of claim.

France

A request for arbitration interrupts the prescription. A request to commence judicial proceedings similarly interrupts the prescription period. The following distinction must be made in respect of the moment when the prescription is interrupted:

(a) In the case of an institutional arbitration (e.g. before the Chambre Arbitrale Maritime of Paris), prescription is interrupted by service to the defendant of a notice to the effect that a request for arbitration has been made to the arbitration institute.
(b) In the case of an *ad hoc* arbitration the prescription is interrupted by the service by the claimant to the defendant of a notice stating that the claimant intends to commence arbitration proceedings, accompanied by the appointment of an arbitrator.

It is not certain that the mere notice of the intention to commence arbitration suffices.

Greece

Pursuant to Article 269 of the Civil Code, the prescription period is interrupted by the submission of the dispute relating to the claim to arbitration (paragraph 1). If for the purpose of submitting the dispute to arbitration it is necessary to appoint arbitrators or to fulfil certain formalities or preconditions, the prescription must be interrupted as soon as the person entitled to rely on the prescription has accomplished whatever was incumbent on him for the settlement of the dispute (paragraph 2).

Ireland

An arbitration shall be deemed to be commenced when one party to the arbitration agreement serves on the other party (or parties) a notice requiring him (or them) to appoint or concur in appointing an arbitrator or, when the arbitration agreement provides that the reference shall be to a person named (or designated) in the agreement, requiring him (or them) to submit the dispute to the person so named and designated.

The commencement of arbitration proceedings operates to prevent the time-bar period running out, (sections 74 and 75 of the Statute of Limitations 1957).

Israel

If the dispute must be submitted to arbitration, the arbitrators, as a rule, are not bound to decide the dispute according to law, and therefore they are also not bound by the legal provisions as to time bar. But if the arbitration agreement provides that the arbitrators shall decide the dispute according to law, the first step taken to start the arbitration proceedings will interrupt the time-bar period (unless it has not already been interrupted by initiating proceedings in court, which have been afterwards referred to arbitration).

Italy

The prescription is interrupted by the notice of appointment of an arbitrator.

Japan

In cases where the arbitration is brought before the Japan Shipping Exchange, Inc. the interruption takes place at the time of application therefor being filed with it.

Korea

An arbitration shall interrupt the prescription period from the time when the application for arbitration has been made.

Malta

If a dispute exists and the parties agree to submit it to arbitration, although there are no decided cases on the subject, it may be argued that the parties would have renounced the prescription period. If there is an arbitration clause, then the normal prescriptive period applies.

Netherlands

If the dispute must be submitted to arbitration by virtue of an arbitral agreement, the running of the time is interrupted at the time the arbitration commences, i.e. on the day of receipt of a written communication by which one party informs the other party of its wish to proceed to arbitration. This communication must contain information concerning the matter which the party resorting to arbitration wishes to submit to arbitration (Code of Civil Procedure, Art. 1025).

One should be aware of the fact that an arbitration clause may refer to rules of arbitration according to which the arbitral proceedings shall commence at a later date, e.g. not until the day of receipt of the request for arbitration by the arbitral tribunal. This is permitted under the law.

Norway

Pursuant to section 14, no. 3 of the Limitation Act, it is sufficient that the claimant does what is required of him according to the arbitration proceedings to get the arbitration under way. Even though any court decisions to this effect cannot be cited, it is commonly considered sufficient that the claimant notifies the other party of appointment of his arbitrator in order to interrupt the time limit. However, if the expiry of the time limit becomes imminent, it may be advisable to issue the points of claim to the arbitrators at the same time as notification of appointment of arbitrators is sent to the other side. The appointed arbitrator must, of course, have accepted the appointment, but it is not necessary to wait for the other side's appointment of an arbitrator and the two arbitrators' agreement on a chairman of the tribunal. If the arbitration agreement should contain provisions to the effect that the case shall be decided by a sole arbitrator, which is rare in Norwegian proceedings, and the arbitration agreement also contains provisions on how this sole arbitrator shall be appointed, it suffices that necessary steps in accordance with the arbitration agreement are taken in order for the appointing body to make an appointment of the sole arbitrator. If the arbitration agreement is ambiguous or an appointment is made which is dependent upon agreement between the parties, it is believed that it will also be possible to apply to the local court for assistance if the other side is not co-operating in having the tribunal or sole arbitrator appointed, when such co-operation is required under the agreement.

Portugal

The prescription is interrupted by the stipulation of the arbitration agreement (Article 324, No. 1 of the Civil Code).

When there is an arbitration clause or the arbitration is imposed by law, the prescription is interrupted through service of process or notice of the appointment of the arbitrator (Article 324, No. 2 of the Civil Code).

Spain

There are no express provisions for prescription in the law of arbitration (Law 36/1988, 5 December 1988, on Arbitration). But it is clear that a simple notice to the debtor announcing the appointment of arbitrator interrupts prescription whenever the civil code rules apply (because this will be deemed to be an extrajudicial claim (see page 189 above).

The situation is rather different as far as the commercial code is concerned. Here the extrajudicial claim is not recognised as a cause of interruption. But any act of recognition of the debt made by the debtor is recognised (see pages 192–193 above). Therefore, any act by the debtor accepting the arbitration procedure for appointment of an arbitrator will interrupt the prescription (this act may be any letter or any other means of communication which leaves a documented proof of the will to submit the claim to arbitration (see Article 6 of Law 36/1988)).

Sweden

The running of the time-bar/extinction period is interrupted in the case of arbitration at such time when one party applies to the other party for a specified topic to be referred to arbitration.

Switzerland

The prescription is interrupted by initiating the procedure for the constitution of the arbitral tribunal (i.e. by appointing the first arbitrator) and by submitting together with the appointment of the arbitrator the request specifying the nature and amount of the claim.

Turkey

The time-bar periods (prescription and extinction periods) are interrupted by commencement of arbitration proceedings.

United Kingdom

In an arbitration, time stops running when:

(i) one party serves notice on the other requiring him to appoint an arbitrator or
(ii) when an arbitrator is specified in the agreement, when one party serves notice on the other requiring him to submit the dispute to the designated arbitrator (Limitation Act 1980, s. 34(3)).

Where an arbitration agreement provides that any claim to which the agreement applies shall be barred unless the arbitration is commenced within a time fixed by the agreement, the Court can extend time if it is of the opinion that undue hardship would otherwise be caused (Arbitration Act 1950, s. 27).

United States

This is generally agreed on by the contracting parties. If the contract does not specify a specific event which tolls the Statute of Limitations, then the running of the time is interrupted when the plaintiff demands arbitration and appoints his/her arbitrator.

6. WHETHER THE COMMENCEMENT OF AN ACTION BEFORE A COURT THAT DOES NOT HAVE JURISDICTION TO DECIDE THE DISPUTE HAS THE EFFECT OF INTERRUPTING THE RUNNING OF THE TIME OR NOT

Argentina

The answer is no. If the claimant is not doing what is necessary to ensure that the proceedings continue in a regular manner and result in a decision of the court, the fact that such proceedings have been commenced in time is not relevant for the purpose of avoiding the lapse of the time-bar period.

Australia

The commencement of an action before a court that does not have jurisdiction to decide the dispute does not interrupt the limitation period, in the sense that "interruption" is defined at page 157. It may constitute commencement of an action within an existing limitation period if the jurisdiction of the court is limited in amount, and if the matter is removed from that court into a court that does not have jurisdiction.

Canada

No, although where a Canadian court does have jurisdiction yet agrees to refer the matter to another court to hear the dispute, a Canadian Court will usually require the defendant to waive any acquired prescription prior to transferring the dispute to such other tribunal.

Chile

If proceedings are commenced before an incompetent court, they do not interrupt the prescription.

China

If the lawsuit is instituted by the claimant in a court having no jurisdiction and the court rejects the case, the time bar period cannot be suspended because it is generally held that the institution of lawsuit as indicated in Article 267 of the Maritime Code refers to bringing a lawsuit in a court having jurisdiction over the case. Moreover, this Article provides that where the lawsuit is rejected, the time-bar period shall not be suspended.

Croatia

The commencement of the action before the court that does not have the jurisdiction to decide the dispute, interrupts the time-bar period provided that the new action has been brought before the competent court no later than three months after the decision by which the previous court declared its incompetence became final (Article 390, paragraph 1 of the Law on Obligations).

Denmark

Danish case law indicates that if an action is commenced before the competent court shortly after having discovered that the court first chosen did not have proper jurisdiction, the action is not time-barred, provided that the incompetent court was chosen in "good faith".

France

Service of proceedings before a tribunal that is lacking jurisdiction interrupts the prescription (Article 2246 of the Civil Code). It would appear that the same conclusion should also hold in the case where an arbitration tribunal declares its lack of jurisdiction.

Germany

The commencement of an action even before a court that does not have jurisdiction has the effect of interrupting the running of the time.

Greece

Pursuant to Article 4 of the Code of Civil Procedure, the filing of an action before a court that does not have jurisdiction to decide the dispute is rejected as inadmissible. Therefore, Article 261 of the Civil Code, which provides that the prescription period is interrupted through the commencement of judicial action, does not apply to such a case and the term of prescription is not interrupted. If the proceedings are abandoned, the prescription is deemed to have never been interrupted.

Ireland

Time is not interrupted by the institution of proceedings before a court that does not have jurisdiction to decide the dispute.

Israel

Lodging the action in a court which is not competent to deal with the case, will probably nevertheless interrupt the time-bar period, as under Israeli law that court is not bound to dismiss the case for lack of jurisdiction, but may refer it to the court which in its opinion is competent in the matter. That court will thereby become competent in the case, even if in its opinion it would not have otherwise been the competent court.

Italy

Commencement of proceedings before a court other than that having venue in respect of the particular claim interrupts prescription. This is expressly stated in Article 2943 of the Civil Code. It is instead debated whether commencement of proceedings before a court lacking jurisdiction has the same effect. The affirmative view has been upheld, with respect to the one-year time limit of Article 3 (6) of the Hague-Visby Rules, by the

Court of Cassation.[25] Proceedings before a court of competent jurisdiction must, however, be commenced within six months from the date of the judgment whereby the jurisdiction was denied.

Japan

Such court is obliged to transfer the action to the court which has jurisdiction over the action (Civil Procedure Act, s 30(1)) so that the effect of interruption arising out of the institution of such action is maintained.

Korea

Even if the suit has been brought before a court which does not have the jurisdiction to decide the dispute, the prescription period is interrupted because the court shall transfer such suit to the competent court by ruling.

Malta

The interruption shall be operative even though the demand, protest, or other judicial act is filed before a court which is not the competent court (section 2129 of the Civil Code). By "competence" here is meant competence *ratione materiae*, i.e. whether proceedings have been commenced before the Commercial or the Civil Court. If the action has been commenced before a court which does not have the jurisdiction to decide the dispute, prescription is not interrupted.

Netherlands

Where an action which has been instituted is not upheld—either on account of the fact that the court does not have jurisdiction or for other reasons—time bar is not interrupted, unless, within six months after the final judgment or other termination of the case, a new action is instituted and is as yet upheld (Civil Code, Art. 3:316).

Norway

An action before the court that does not have jurisdiction will normally have the effect that a one-year time limit is running from the date when the court decided it had no jurisdiction, provided that the claimants did not deliberately elect the wrong court. If the non-competent court should fail to notify the claimant properly about its decision, the one-year time limit will commence to run from the date he actually knew about the dismissal of the case or ought to have asked for information from the court. How-

25. Judgment 18 June 1987, No. 5357 in *S.p.A. Navigazione Alga* v. *S.a.s. Rhin et Moselle*, 1988, Dir. Mar. 1107.

ever, there is an absolute time limit expiring three years after the incompetent court closed the case. Also, a suit abroad may have a similar effect, provided it was reasonable to assume that the foreign court might have jurisdiction in the case.

Portugal

The fact that the court before which the action is brought, is incompetent does not prevent the commencement of another action with the same object. In this case, without prejudice to the statutory provisions, the prescription and the forfeiture of rights, the civil effects due to the commencement of the first action and to the service of the proceedings to the defendant continue whenever possible, if the new action is started or if service of the proceedings to the defendant is made within 30 days from the date when the decision becomes *re judicata* (Article 289 of the Code of Civil Procedure).

Spain

In the case of a judicial action, it is necessary to issue proceedings in a Spanish Court of Law. However, issuing proceedings in a foreign court may be equivalent to "any kind of claim" provided the action has been notified to the debtor, thus interrupting prescription as per the civil code rules. In the same manner, if the debtor acknowledged his debt by any act done in such proceedings, prescription will be interrupted pursuant to the provisions of the commercial code.

If the suit is issued in a Spanish non-competent court and the defendant pleads for a writ of prohibition or for a declinatory exception, he is recognising the debt and thus prescription is interrupted. Less clear is the case where it is the judge himself (*ex officio*) who abstains and gives notice to the plaintiff to exercise his right before the competent court (see Article 74 of the Ley Enjuiciamiento Civil).

Sweden

The running of a time-bar/extinction period may also be interrupted in a case when a claim has been filed with the wrong general court. The Court of Appeal may then, upon the request of one party, arrange for the case to be transferred to the correct forum. It is unclear whether the same applies for special cases to be referred exclusively to certain courts.

Switzerland

The general provision of Article 139 of the Code of Obligations provides for an additional time of 60 days to file or commence an action before the competent court in cases where the prescription period would otherwise have expired in the meantime. Only the correct action will cause the prescription period to be interrupted. There are Cantonal provisions of civil procedure which will request the court having no jurisdiction to transfer the case to the competent court. In such cases the action brought before the incorrect court has already the effect of interrupting the prescription period.

Turkey

Time is not interrupted in such circumstances. But pursuant to Article 137 of the Code of Obligations if the action or the plea is refused to be entertained for the reasons as to competency or lack of formality and meanwhile the prescription period expires, the claimant benefits from an additional 60 days.

United Kingdom

In order to interrupt the running of time it is necessary to issue proceedings in a United Kingdom court of law.[26]

United States

Generally, the commencement of an action before a court that does not have jurisdiction to decide the dispute will not interrupt the running of the time.[27] However, under the doctrine of equitable tolling, "tolling is appropriate" even when filed in a court lacking jurisdiction, when "there exists a reasonable legal theory for invoking the jurisdiction of the court".[28]

7. WHETHER IN A CASE OF A PROCEEDING BEING ABANDONED OR DISCONTINUED, THE TIME COMMENCES TO RUN AGAIN AND, IF SO, FROM WHEN

Australia

Abandonment or discontinuance of proceedings does not start time running again.

26. As accepted in *The Spiliada* [1987] 1 Lloyd's Rep. 1.
27. 54 Corpus Juris Secundum, paragraph 220.
28. *Fox* v. *Eaton Corp.*, 615 F.2d 716, 719 (6th Cir. 1980).

Canada

If the action is discontinued, it is deemed never to have been taken and its commencement would not be taken as having affected the running of time. If the action is abandoned, this is not a formal step and would have no consequence until there was a formal discontinuance or continuing of the action.

China

Article 267 of the Maritime Code provides that if the claimant withdraws the lawsuit or the lawsuit is rejected by the court, the time-bar period shall not be suspended.

Croatia

In the case of the proceedings being abandoned the time-bar period is not interrupted (Article 389, paragraph 1 of the Law of Obligations 1978). In cases where the period is interrupted the time commences to run again and the time elapsed does not affect the length of time-bar periods as provided by the law (Article 392, paragraph 1 of the Law on Obligations 1978).

Denmark

In such cases the time does not commence to run again.

France

Two situations must be considered:

(i) That of one party discontinuing the proceedings with the consent of the other party. In such case, a new prescription period commences to run from the time the discontinuance becomes effective, *viz.* from the time, normally, when discontinuance is accepted by the defendant (such acceptance is not necessary if the defendant has not filed any defence on the merits: Article 395 of the Nouveau Code de procédure civile).

(ii) Interruption of proceedings during a period of two years acknowledged by the judge (peremption). In such a case, all effects of the previous proceedings, including the service of proceedings, is annulled retroactively. As a consequence of that, a further distinction must be drawn.

(a) the initial prescription period (e.g. that of two years in maritime matters) has matured: in such a case the prescription is definitive.

(b) the initial prescription period has not matured yet (e.g. the 10-year period for damages to the environment by pollution by hydrocarbons). In such a case a new prescription period commences to run from the date of the acknowledgement of the extinction by the judge.

Germany

In the cases mentioned above the time continues to run as if no interruption had occurred.

Ireland

In such a case time would commence to run on the date of the original accrual of the cause of action. Thus if a writ is issued within the required time and not properly continued, and a fresh originating summons is afterwards issued on which the Plaintiff proceeds, the commencement of the action is the issuing of the last originating summons, and if this is out of time the claimant is barred.

In certain circumstances the court may allow the claimant to amend the originating summons after the relevant period of limitation has expired. In such circumstances, time ceases to run on the date of the issue of the original unamended originating summons.

Israel

If the case has been dismissed in a manner which would not prevent the plantiff from suing again, the limitation period will be deemed to be suspended from the time the action has been instituted until its dismissal; for instance, if the court dismisses the action following its discontinuance by the plaintiff and if the right to bring a fresh action is reserved in the judgment.

Italy

Pursuant to Article 2945 of the Civil Code in case of extinction of the proceedings a new prescription period commences from the date of the interruption, *viz.* from the date when proceedings commenced.

Japan

If the action is dismissed or withdrawn, such demand does not have the effect of interrupting the period from the date when the demand is made (Civil Code, s. 149).

Korea

A demand by way of judicial proceedings shall not have the effect of interrupting prescription, if the action is dismissed, intervention in bankruptcy proceedings, attachment or provisional attachment, or provisional disposition is made within six months, the prescription shall be deemed to have been retroactively interrupted from the time of the demand by way of the first judicial proceedings (Article 170 of the Civil Code).

Malta

The interruption of prescription made by means of a judicial demand shall be deemed inoperative if the plaintiff withdraws the action or if the action is deserted, or dismissed (section 2132(1) of the Civil Code). However, the withdrawal of dismissal of the action must refer to the merit of the demand, because if the plaintiff simply renounces the acts or if the judgment simply discharges the defendant *ab observantia judicii*, in other words, if the plaintiff can, according to law, reinstitute the action, provided such action is reinstituted before the same or another court within one month from the day of its previous withdrawal or dismissal, and service thereof is effected before the expiration of one month from the last day of the period of prescription, the interruption will be operative (section 2132(2) of the Civil Code). If these conditions concur, the reinstitution of the demand does not operate interruption *ex novo* but it merely gives effect to the original interruption, which, therefore, remains operative even though the action is reinstituted after the expiration of the period of prescription.

Netherlands

Where an action or other act of judicial recourse is withdrawn, the time bar is not interrupted, i.e. interruption is deemed not to have taken place at any time.

Norway

If the claimant is abandoning or discontinuing the proceedings, the claim will normally become time-barred if the period has already expired. Only if the court acknowledges the claim or a settlement in court is reached, or a similar decision on the substance of the claim is arrived at, will a new time limit of 10 years commence to run. If the proceedings are discontinued because the court lacks jurisdiction or for other reasons (in other words: if a decision is made closing the proceedings without deciding on the substantive issue) then what is stated at page 192 above will apply.

Once proceedings are commenced, it is not only up to the plaintiff to decide whether the proceeding shall be brought to an end or not. If the plaintiff withdraws the proceedings, he cannot do so without at the same time withdrawing the claim as such. If so, he has, of course, waived the claim, and no further question of time bar will arise. The defendant is in such cases also entitled to ask for costs, and the plaintiff is obliged to pay the defendant's costs in full. If the claimant is not interested in continuing the proceedings, he may, of course, *de facto*, discontinue them by not filing any further application or pleadings to the court, but if so, the defendant is entitled to ask the court to fix a date for the hearing and decide the case on its merits. If the defendant elects to remain passive, the court will simply fix a date for the hearing and pass a judgment on the basis of what transpires during the hearing. A judgment by default may also be passed if one of the parties does not appear. The situation described in this question is, therefore, not relevant under Norwegian law.

Spain

General statutory provisions in respect of interruption of the prescription are contained in Article 1973 of the Civil Code.

Special rules for interruption of contractual commercial obligations and for collision, are specified in Article 944 of the Commercial Code.

Besides, special rules provided in maritime international conventions have to be taken into account.

In the Civil Code regime any act by which the action is exercised in a judicial proceeding interrupts prescription (Article 1973). A claim made to the judge suffices. Proceeding is deemed to be commenced not only with the formal commencement of a lawsuit. Requesting to the judge a simple act of conciliation will suffice.

The Commercial Code seems to establish a very similar regime. Prescrition is interrupted by commencement of a lawsuit or by any other kind of judicial claim made to the debtor. However, interruption does not occur if the suit is not admitted, it the plaintiff discontinues the action or if the proceeding is extinguished pursuant to the rules of Procedural Law (see Article 944 of the Commercial Code and Article 411 *et seq*. of the Ley de Enjuiciamiento Civil).

Sweden

In cases where a proceeding becomes abandoned or discontinued the time bar will not be considered to have been interrupted at all.

Switzerland

The time interrupted starts to run immediately after each and every step causing such an interruption.

Turkey

In the cases mentioned above, a new prescription period commences to run from the date of abandonment or discontinuance of proceedings pursuant to Article 136 of the Code of Obligations.

United Kingdom

Where a plaintiff has discontinued an action or withdrawn a claim, he may nevertheless commence a new action for the same cause at a subsequent date (see RSC Ord. 21, R. 4). However, the new action must be brought within good time; otherwise his laches might become a bar.[29]

Where leave is required to discontinue or withdraw, the court has a discretion to impose a term that no other action may be brought.

United States

In the absence of a statute to the contrary, a party cannot deduct from the period of a Statute of Limitations the time during which an action subsequently voluntarily dismissed was pending.[30]

29. See *Reid* v. *London & N. Staffs Insurance Co.* (1883) 49 L.T. 468.
30. 54 Corpus Juris Secundum, para. 249.

INDEX